Tips to Find Happiness

Tips to Find Happiness

Creating a Harmonious Home for Your Spouse,
Your Children, and Yourself

●

Ryuho Okawa

Lantern Books • New York

A Division of Booklight Inc.

Lantern Books
A Division of Booklight Inc.
Lantern Books
128 Second Place
Brooklyn, NY 11231
www.lanternbooks.com

Printed in the United States of America

ISBN: 978-1-59056-315-1
Earlier edition appeared under ISBN: 1-59056-080-9

MIX
Paper from
responsible sources
FSC
www.fsc.org   FSC® C011935

Table of Contents

Preface vii

Chapter One: Your Work and Family
1. How to Behave toward a Father Exhausted by Work 1
2. Be Caring When Your Partner Is Unwell 4
3. How to Survive Difficult Times 6
4. How to Overcome Ordeals and Continue Growing 10

Chapter Two: Your Family Relationships
1. When a Partner Lacks Ambition 13
2. The Causes of Domestic Violence
   and How to Deal with It 16
3. How to Recover from a Divorce 22
4. How to Avoid the Danger of Divorce Later in Life 26

Chapter Three: Your Children
1. How to Raise Gifted Children 30
2. A Method of Developing a Child's Gifts 34
3. Parents Should Work with Their Children to
   Prevent Delinquency and Absence from School 38
4. For Children with Physical Disabilities 41
5. How to Deal with Children Addicted to Video Games 44
6. Religious Education to Encourage
   a Right Way of Living 47
7. Religious Education Is Needed to Prevent Delinquency .. 50

Chapter Four: Creating a Happier Family

1. Making the Home Happier 53
2. The Secret of a Wonderful Old Age 59
3. Diet and Control of the Mind 63
4. The Effect of the Brain and the Soul
   on the Intellect 65
5. It Is Possible to Overcome Hereditary Diseases 68
6. A Happy Household Can Prevent Child Abuse 71
7. Secrets for Overcoming a Short Temper
   and Developing Patience 75
8. How to Expand Your Capacity to Love 77

Postscript 83

About the Author 85

Lantern Books by Ryuho Okawa 87

What is Happy Science? 89

Contacts 93

Want to Know More? 95

Preface

The series of question-and-answer sessions entitled "A Compass for Life" was first published in our monthly magazine, and was well-received by readers. To questions on many different topics asked at different times, I have offered advice, sometimes in the form of clear-cut solutions to problems, and at other times in the form of koans for Zen meditation.[1] I tried to answer these questions in the best way, considering each one to be a once-in-a-lifetime opportunity. I have presented the Truth in a way that is appropriate to the recipient. Faced with the same question from a different person at a different time, I am sure that my answer would take an entirely different form.

In this book, I have selected themes from the Q&A sessions that have a bearing on happiness in the home. It is a collection of hints to keep to hand in every home, or carry with you at any time. If you read this book, I am sure you will find what I say to be helpful. I have selected the contents of this book myself, and I have every confidence they will be of help to readers. If you find it offers solutions to the problems you are facing in your life, please recommend it to your friends and acquaintances.

Ryuho Okawa
Founder and CEO
Happy Science Group

---

[1] A koan is a short question that is like a riddle, to be contemplated in self-reflection or meditation.

Chapter One

Your Work and Family

1. How to Behave toward a Father Exhausted by Work

Question: *My father seems to think himself worthy of respect, but in my eyes he is not; he drinks too much, he shouts a lot and is very critical of others. As his daughter, I feel that he suffers a powerful sense of unhappiness and is unable to see himself objectively. This being the case, how should I try to relate to him?*

Wounded pride from past setbacks

It seems that you do not see the whole picture when it comes to your father. You may be incapable of understanding the feelings of someone who has suffered numerous unhappy experiences out in the world over a period of several decades. I imagine the reason for this is that you do not have the necessary knowledge of the world of business.

From the little you have told me in your question, I believe I can understand why your father behaves as he does. I am not alone in this; I suppose that anyone with some experience of working in the business world will sympathize with the way he feels. He has probably suffered some major setback. He is basically a proud man but experience has wounded his pride—I am sure this is the case. He doubtless feels he has been treated badly by a superior or a colleague, and the results of his work have often been disappointing.[1]

When proud, confident people suffer a blow to their pride like this, they often feel that they have to compensate for it in some way; however, at the same time, they do not want others to realize that they have been hurt. This can manifest in a variety of ways, but most typically the person who has been injured becomes aggressive, abusing others and criticizing their environment. This is a very common pattern of behavior. In this way, people try to preserve their pride. They think they can compensate for wounded pride by finding fault with others.

Although such people may realize that the problem lies with themselves, they are reluctant to admit this and do not want others to point it out to them. This results in their becoming very critical of others. Your father's tendency to drink too much stems from a strong desire to deceive himself. People who drink too much generally do so because they wish to suppress their rational faculty, and are eager to escape. They want to escape from reality, they do not want to face the facts, and in most cases, the reality they are trying to avoid is a negative self-image. In an effort to escape from a poor self-image, they turn to drink.

---

[1] In the process of numerous incarnations, a soul that was male in the previous life can be born as a woman in the next life on Earth, and vice versa. The human soul is essentially a spiritual energy that transcends gender; when it takes on a physical form, it chooses the gender most suited to learning or to the mission on Earth.

Believe in your father's goodness

It is not always a good idea to make these sorts of people look objectively at their own faults. On the contrary, it is more effective to praise their strengths. A man whose pride has been hurt can be very much like a wounded lion; he is dangerous and it is better that you help him somehow compensate for his injury. After that, just leave him alone; do not criticize him. No matter what he may say, just let it flow over you, telling yourself that the storm will pass eventually.

Your father's behavior is common, and in many cases people who suffer as a result of their pride have great potential. People who do not cherish high ideals usually do not suffer greatly when they face setbacks. However, those who suffer in this way may create disturbances or be rude to others when they are drunk, temporarily seeming to be the worst sort of person. However, in many cases they are actually intelligent, able people. Because this is the case, they suffer much pain and anguish.

It is best if such people use their pain and disappointment as a springboard from which to move in the right direction; however, if their wounds cause them to move in the opposite direction, their lives will be filled with despair. To prevent this from happening, it is vital that the people around them are considerate of them, and make sure that they do not become resigned to failure. What is most important at this time is the power of love. The best way is to believe in your father. Believe that at heart he is a wonderful person.

Daughters are strongly influenced by their parents, and it is rarely the case that someone worthy of respect has hopeless parents. If you are a wonderful woman, then it can be assumed that your parents are wonderful people, too. Please focus more on your father's good points.

2. Be Caring When Your Partner Is Unwell

Question: *My husband is in his early fifties and is currently manager of the sales department of his company. He has done well at work but over the last few years he has suffered from a bad back, rashes and numerous other maladies. He has had two operations to remove tumors. As a result of retinal disease from diabetes he has also largely lost his eyesight and the doctor says anyone else would have given up their job. What should I do to help him?*

Illnesses in sales people are "honorable wounds"

People who work in sales live by their nerves and they are often prone to illness. Just what kind of illness they suffer varies from person to person, but whatever it is, it will be a result of stress. A sales manager is sure to overexert himself somehow, working late and entertaining clients, particularly as a section chief or manager in his forties; he will have pushed himself beyond his limits.

For this reason, those who have made a career for themselves in sales are sure to suffer ill-health and their illnesses could be looked on as "honorable wounds." These people worked hard to achieve success, and as a result, they have fallen ill. Working for a company is tough. However, some people have no choice but to continue working, although they may feel that they would like to leave their job.

Try to understand your partner's pain
and make your home comfortable

For many years your partner has overextended himself at work and now the accumulated exhaustion and stress have damaged his body, so the first thing you will need to do for him is to express your understanding that he has made a great effort up to now.

Next, to allow him to work as long as possible, make the home a comfortable place where he will be able to relax and get over the stress he suffers. It is a good idea to try to make him rest. Having devoted himself wholeheartedly to his job, he will not have rested when he should, always pushing himself to the limits; however, the human body can only take so much punishment. A wise person will see to it that their partner takes a rest before he or she overdoes it.

Watch your partner carefully and when you think his work is getting on top of him, apply the brakes and force him to rest. He is exhausted and wounded by years of work so try to supply peace of mind. Be careful not to be too forceful or nag as this will only cause him to resist; rather, try to ask yourself what you can do to help him relax and recover from his stress.

I assume that if he is able to have a good rest, his health will improve. However, if it has deteriorated beyond repair, a better option may be to persuade him to end his current career and look for a less demanding job. Basically, his body is beginning to deteriorate and medical treatment alone will not be sufficient to achieve a cure. However, it is often the case that merely the attempt to understand and appreciate a partner for his long years of hard work is sufficient to bring about his recovery.

You will also find that spiritual techniques such as self-reflection, meditation and prayer are effective. For help with this, please feel free to visit your local branch or meditation center at the Happy Science where you will find "Prayers to Cure Illness," and other prayers and seminars.

3. How to Survive Difficult Times

Question: *At times when I am filled with pain or sorrow, I cannot help feeling I have a lot of faults and I lose confidence in myself as a leader who can inspire others. What kind of attitude should I adopt at such times?*

Humility and compassion are born of sorrow

It is possible to regard pain and sorrow as negative emotions rather than emotions from heaven, and this tendency is particularly strong in the Japanese Shinto religion. However, there is another aspect that should not be overlooked, that pain and sorrow also have the effect of lending depth to a person's character.

People who have suffered deep sorrow will benefit in the following two ways. Firstly, they will have learned humility. Sadness caused by injured pride will allow them to learn the true meaning of humility.

Secondly, they will be kind to others. If they cannot empathize with others, they will scarcely be able to express compassion toward them. Those who are blessed by good circumstances and whose lives are proceeding smoothly in particular have a tendency to be severe toward others. Their speech becomes harsh and they condemn other people, making remarks such as: "Can't you even do a simple thing like that?"

However, once people have experienced deep sorrow themselves, they will have a greater capacity to forgive others because they understand others' grief as if it were their own. This is something that can only be gained through experience.

People who have experienced sorrow possess a unique form of compassion. It is a form of light. This is what is meant by the saying: "When you break through the bottom of sorrow, light floods out." The chief characteristics of those who have passed through great sadness are a gentle gaze upon others and a willingness to wait patiently for others' growth. Those who have difficulty forgiving need to consider whether or not they have ever experienced any deep sorrow or disappointment.

Pain tempers the soul and develops generosity

Another emotion that resembles sorrow is pain. These two feelings are like twins. Pain also has a positive side; it serves to strengthen the soul. Without pain, the soul stagnates; a life that just passes smoothly will not help develop a deep refinement of character. A soul that has been tempered by pain expresses itself in a character that is well-developed. Pain develops a breadth of character and creates a greater capacity to embrace others. A variety of painful experiences will serve to increase the stature of a soul.

Instead of seeing sorrow and pain simply as negative, it is important to see them as opportunities for awakening to a deeper understanding of the Truth. It is through sorrow and pain that the range and depth of human understanding grow.

Become able to understand the feelings of others

From olden times it has been said that in order to achieve greatness, a person must experience poverty, the loss of a job, demotion, a broken heart, the break up of a marriage, or illness. Failing exams, being kept back a year at school, a failed relationship or business can also be added to the list.

People who experience one of these traumas tend to become rather introverted, but once they overcome the setback, they emit a deep light. These people are able to empathize deeply with the finer feelings of others, so the way in which they perceive and interact with another can in itself be an act of forgiveness.

Everyone has wounds to their heart that hurt if touched. However, when someone who has never suffered sees a person who is wounded, they callously rub salt into the wounds. Through their words and actions they add to the hurt of the other person. Someone who has experienced pain or failure themselves will understand the pain caused by rubbing salt into a wound. Those who have not are unable to sympathize and as soon as they find a fault or a failing in another, they will not hesitate to make the pain worse. In some cases, they will want to cause others the kind of harm that can affect them badly and cause permanent damage.

When people are suffering with some problem and they still have not reached rock bottom, it can sometimes bring a sense of contentment to pick on someone else and find fault with another, as if picking on someone helps them to keep their own head above water. Many people cannot stop themselves from acting in this way even though it is the worst kind of pleasure; finding fault or criticizing others is the very lowest form of gratification.

People who think that they can alleviate their own pain by picking on others still do not know true pain. Those who truly suffer pain and struggle to find the true self cannot obtain relief simply by pointing out the faults of others. They need to temper themselves further until finally they develop true kindness. In other words, as long as you find yourself picking on others, blaming or criticizing them, it means that your character still requires further deepening and that you still do not know true sorrow or pain.

People who have passed through the worst that life can offer will become truly kind and incapable of doing anything that hurts others because they themselves have suffered having their own wounds probed. This attitude is a form of forgiveness. Forgiveness is not limited to forgiving others' faults. When you pass through sorrow or pain, your capacity for forgiveness will grow, and this is a positive outcome of sorrow or pain.

Let the fountain of love overflow

It is hard for people to hide their true character. Someone in whom the "fountain of love" gushes forth will find that all kinds of people gather round to receive their blessings. Conversely, someone who takes pleasure in the pain of others will not attract people to them. By observing yourself from this perspective, it is easy to learn which group you belong to. Someone whom others frequently approach, wanting to discuss their problems, is someone in whom the fountain of love is abundant, while those whom others shun are people in whom the fountain of love has dried up.

You may believe that once you have realized your own shortcomings, you will no longer be able to exert a positive influence on others. However, the best you can do is to aim for love to flow naturally from within you. If you endeavor to deepen your enlightenment, you will find that, in the process, the fountain of love within will naturally begin to overflow. Proof of this can be found in the fact that people automatically gather round a person on account of their virtue, in much the same way as described in the Chinese proverb that says, "Although the peach trees and the plum trees remain silent, people gather beneath them for their blossoms and their fruit."

If you look at others with a critical eye, they will be afraid of having their shortcomings pointed out or being told off, so they will not approach you. If you give off an air of kindness, people will naturally congregate in your vicinity. It is a mysterious phenomenon; in a sense, it can be said that everyone has spiritual powers. The same is true in business—a shop that always seems to be experiencing hard times will fail to attract customers, while a shop that exudes a certain freshness like a warm spring wind will always attract a lot of business.

So before you worry about having a positive influence on others, dig a well within yourself. As the water flows from this well, you will find that sheep will automatically flock to you and drink from your spring. Only when this happens can you lead others, like a shepherd. However, if you try to coerce others into following you, you will find that you have become like a wolf. If you use force, the sheep will look on you as a wolf and flee from your presence. Instead, it is important to allow the waters to well up naturally. Then the sheep will flock around and this will give you confidence.

4. How to Overcome Ordeals and Continue Growing

Question: *In life we are confronted with numerous ordeals; what kind of attitude do we need to adopt when we face one?*

Be thankful for any ordeal

It is true that in the course of our lives we are confronted by times that seem to shake us to our very foundations. However, we must realize that we are on Earth to undergo spiritual refinement and to strengthen our souls, and it is for this reason we are faced with a wide range of experiences.

So when you face worries, remind yourself that you are undergoing a period of growth, that you have been confronted by this particular test in order to allow you to grow, and give thanks for it. When you are presented with an ordeal, when you are faced with a problem that seems too difficult to overcome, the first thing you should do is to fill your heart with a sense of gratitude.

God never gives you too much to bear

God never confronts a person with a problem that is too difficult for them to solve; it is something that He has never done and never will. The person who is struggling may believe that he or she is incapable of coping with the load, but in God's eyes it is exactly the right size.

To explain this, let me take the example of a man who is carrying luggage on his back. In actual fact this man is capable of carrying heavy loads but he avoids them and only carries the lighter ones. Eventually, he is given extra weight, which makes him think he will be crushed by it. However, although the load is heavy on his back, he remains upright and realizes that he is all right. After walking for a while, another load is placed on him. Once more he is convinced that he will collapse, but he does not. At last he realizes that even though he believed himself to be incapable of carrying such a heavy load, in actual fact he is able to, and he was just not making enough effort.

The same also happens at work. As the workload increases, people may worry and feel they cannot handle it, but the truth is that God knows that they are still capable of taking more. So when you feel that you have reached your limits, it is important to tell yourself that it is only that you probably still have not done all the work that God expects of you, and you are capable of taking more and managing it successfully.

As you develop, difficult problems no longer seem overwhelming

As you grow, you sometimes find that what once appeared to you to be major issues too difficult to solve become really quite minor, not even worth worrying about. For instance, when a company suddenly undergoes a period of massive growth, the staff may feel that they are unable to cope with the changes this creates or to keep up. However, as they struggle to handle their increased workload, they discover that up until this time they have not been making sufficient effort and they have been panicking over nothing. People sometimes believe that they are facing an insurmountable problem when in truth it is only in their own imagination.

Believe that although you may feel you are now facing a problem that you are incapable of overcoming, in a year's time you should be able to solve it for yourself. Therefore, think what you would do if you looked at it in a year's time, and I am sure you will find a solution. In other words, imagine how you will be in the future, how you will have developed, and then bring this image back into the present. If you do this, you will find that you have become stronger. I believe it is worth trying.

Sometimes it happens that while you are struggling with a problem, you find that the problem has already solved itself without your realizing it. At first you may think that it is unbelievable that you have been able to solve such a difficult problem, but soon you will find that you no longer need to give that problem a second thought.

Chapter Two

Your Family Relationships

1. When a Partner Lacks Ambition

Question: *Several years ago I married and my husband and I have two children. However, my husband has not been working for a long time and recently he seems to be suffering from depression. Please tell me what I need to do to help him get back on his feet.*

The subconscious of the strong-willed
Traditionally it has been considered a man's responsibility to support his family, so a man who is incapable of doing this could be considered by society as unfit to marry and have children. A man must be aware of his responsibilities. However, your husband is probably lacking an awareness of his responsibilities. I do not know how you feel about this, but I presume that you tend to be attracted to this kind of man or that subconsciously you feel incapable of realizing your dreams unless you are with a man of this type.

It is a strange thing but strong-willed, independent women have a tendency to marry weak men. An energetic woman can often be found with a man who has little drive. About ten percent of women fall into this category; they are full of energy and derive pleasure from supporting their man. They may complain and ask why their husband is so useless, but subconsciously they feel that this man's very existence is what gives their lives purpose. It is important to ask yourself what you feel subconsciously.

Stop competing with your spouse

The truth of the matter is that your husband has become the way he is partly because of something in you. Although they may not be aware of it themselves, some women subconsciously resent their gender, wishing they had been born men. When these women marry, they unconsciously set about bringing their husbands down.

This is particularly true when a husband and wife compete with each other and the wife overtakes her husband. For example, if the wife is more intelligent than her husband, if she comes from a better family, if she is the daughter of a wealthy man while her husband is poor, or if she is outstandingly beautiful while her husband's looks are only average, this will trigger various failures for him.

When this happens she will feel that she has made a great sacrifice, that she has given him a precious diamond and received little in return. In a situation like this, where she believes herself to be of greater value than her husband, the man will often resort to escapism; he will leave home, have affairs or lose his job. This is partly because he craves love, but it is also a result of the fact that although he wants to be admired by his partner, he fails to achieve this, so he reacts like a child who refuses to go to school, expressing himself in a negative way that brings trouble to the family.

You need to look back at your thoughts and deeds from the time of your wedding onward and tell yourself that part of the responsibility lies with you. After that, pray that your husband will change and move in the direction of your ideals. Even though you may think that you are praying, if you are subconsciously working to bring him down it will not do any good. Bring your conscious and subconscious into harmony, and with sincerity form a clear image of your ideal for your husband, then pray for this to be realized.

Strengthen your inner light and deepen your spiritual awareness

It is also necessary to transform yourself so that your heart is gentle and you overflow with love. It is very likely that your husband has come under negative spiritual influences. When a husband, a wife or children are under these sorts of spiritual influences, it is possible that they can be conquered through love. If the household becomes happier, the spirits that are affecting you negatively cannot help but go away. If these spirits are able to sneak in and take over your family, it means that there is still not enough light there.

So, start by speaking kindly and lovingly. Next, train yourself to look at your family rightly, with an objective eye. Although the order is different to that of the Noble Eightfold Path, which traditional Buddhism teaches, practicing Right Speech and Right View in this way will allow you to find that the situation will change significantly. After that, it depends on the extent to which you are able to deepen your spiritual awareness. In a sense, your husband is currently acting as a whetstone on which you can refine and strengthen your soul. Because of his presence your spiritual awareness can be deepened and for this you can be thankful.

People are born on Earth to undergo spiritual refinement and everyone in this world is given particular challenges to overcome. Different people have been given a different workbook of problems to be solved, and yours contains the issue you now struggle with. The way in which you go about solving this will add to your capabilities. You will not be faced with the same problems as other people, and it is important you tackle your own problems head on. No one else can solve your problems, so please help yourself and strive to overcome them on your own. You are sure to find a solution in the end.

2. The Causes of Domestic Violence and How to Deal with It

Question: *Why does domestic violence occur? Please tell me what causes it and how it should be dealt with.*

The chain of stress within the family

We are experiencing a decline in the current economic climate and it is only natural that this should bring with it various forms of stress. In offices, a person may have difficulty expressing their potential through work, but other family members have no way of knowing what that person is doing at work—what kind of mistakes they make or whether they are being reprimanded by a manager.

In the good old days, men used to bring home a wage packet and for this reason they were respected and appreciated in the home, but now that wages are transferred directly to an individual's bank account, men are no longer treated with the same respect, and in many cases, have become almost like lodgers in their own homes. With the recent dearth of overtime, fathers return home much earlier and some of them may display violence toward their families. On the other hand, others may express their dissatisfaction at constantly having to work overtime through violence within the family. It is probable that these people are suffering some kind of stress and they take it out on those closest to them.

Some mothers may take jobs out of the necessity to earn extra income while others may devote themselves to success at work. However, there are limits to a person's capabilities and it is difficult to earn a monthly wage and still manage to see to all the housework alone perfectly. The extra work will exhaust mothers, resulting in a kind of emotional instability.

What about the children? Some children come from homes that are disturbed, while others suffer as a result of disruption at school. Children who come from troubled families will often misbehave at school, becoming violent, not doing what they are told, bullying other children and causing endless trouble. If we look at children who bully others, we see that some of them come from homes where their parents are on the verge of divorce. They find the situation hard to bear and vent their frustration at school.

In this way, unhappiness can spread like wildfire, causing a negative chain reaction. We are currently in a situation where the smoke of new fires is springing up all around.

Do not rely on external help, instead effect change from within

In the current situation, you may well be disappointed if you look to the outside for help in changing your environment. Things at the office may not always go as well as they did in the past and you will not be able to earn a lot doing some simple job. The same can be said of children. Just because they go to a good school does not mean they can expect to enter a good university, or be guaranteed the career of their dreams.

In these times, everyone is suffering some kind of frustration, feeling blocked off. This means that it is pointless to look for help from the outside. The only way out is to change within, to change yourself from inside.

Develop a calm mind and persevere, pursuing lofty ideals

What is important when changing from within? In the case of violence or physical abuse between a husband and wife, or parents and children, the people involved often do not realize that they are doing anything wrong. When they become violent, they feel a release, and their stress is lessened. If they were to be violent outside the home, they would be likely to get into trouble, but inside the home, to a certain extent, the family will put up with it. So, often violence is used unconsciously as a way of reducing stress.

However, resorting to violence indicates that every other method of reducing stress in the home has been exhausted. The home should be a place where people are able to unwind and soothe away the cares of daily life. Today, however, the home itself has become filled with stress and people can no longer do this. Someone whose stress has been passed on from another family member will not be able to bear it; they will try to give it to someone else. In this way, the whole family projects their stress onto one another and the wounds become deeper.

To overcome this vicious cycle, it is important to cultivate perseverance and a peaceful heart. What is required is the effort to erase the petty conflicts and worries of this world from your mind, and to this end it is beneficial to have an interest in the Truth, to seek higher aims and loftier ideals. This is a way of solving a problem, by replacing worries with something more positive. The human mind is incapable of thinking about two things at the same time, and in some respects, this is a blessing. For instance, someone who is manic-depressive can only be manic or depressed; they cannot be both at the same time. In the same way, people cannot hold two thoughts in their mind at once. This is a human limitation, to be able to hold only one thought at a time. We are also unable to do a number of things simultaneously.

The fact that people are only able to think of one thing at a time can be a blessing. If you are absorbed in one subject, or trying to distract your mind, it saves you from thinking about anything else. So, one way to reduce stress is to direct your thoughts to something higher.

Finding joy in the home

In the near future we can hardly expect much improvement in the socio-economic conditions and it is going to become increasingly difficult to achieve promotion or success. For this reason it is better to try to find happiness in the home. This is a period of corporate restructuring and deflation, but simultaneously it is a time when people can rediscover the value of the family. We are experiencing a change in era, where people are returning home earlier, and returning to a simpler life reminiscent of several decades ago.

It would be better for people to adopt values that are slightly different, more traditional. It would be a good idea to do things with the families that they have never done together before. They can try to think of enjoyable activities that do not cost much, things they have not done for ten or twenty years. For instance when a couple were newlyweds perhaps they liked to go out together to have coffee, to take walks or buy flowers to decorate the house—small things like this, which ten or twenty years of marriage have driven from their minds. They can return to simple hobbies or pastimes like these that cost little to enjoy.

If there are children in your home who have been neglected due to the pressures of work, then you can look for value in the simple things you can do with them. I am sure that there are many parents who have always been too busy with work to go and watch their children's events. However, if you have enough free time, you can be grateful and use this to deepen your relationship with your family. You can go and watch your children in plays, visit exhibitions displaying their work, or even help them with their homework—there are any number of things you can do to help develop your relationship with your children.

Bring peace to your heart
The period we are about to enter will call for changes in our sense of values. We must not just give up; rather, we can take this opportunity to focus on what is within, slowly building our strength while we await the chance to make a comeback.

Now is the time to find peace of mind, something forgotten in the past. The fact that parents and children can be together at weekends is a good thing. There are lots of things a family can do together over the weekend. With no work at weekends and the children at home, there are lots of enjoyable activities you can do; the whole family can go and spend a peaceful time at a branch or meditation center of Happy Science.

It is important that you change your values and become aware of things you have never noticed before. It is good to carve a new way through effort, but if you find that a path will not open despite trying, then the Taoist philosophies may be beneficial. Buddhism is also helpful because there is an aspect of withdrawal from everyday life to it. Violence is something that should be avoided, but its roots are always within the heart of the individual, so first it is important to look squarely within.

Knowing how to be content

Another attitude that is necessary in this age is knowing how to be content. Neither society nor the individual can easily succeed in new achievements as rapidly as in the past. Overall, wages will be stagnant and those who work in offices will be assessed more rigorously.

It is important to know how to be content and to make an effort to discover joy in the small things. For example, you can be grateful merely for the fact that you have a job, or that your children are able to go to school. Even though your children may not manage to achieve anything remarkable, you can be grateful for the fact that you are able to afford to send them to extra-curricular music lessons or sport. If the parents have lost their jobs, the children have to give up lessons in subjects not taught at school. Even if you cannot afford these, and even if your children's classrooms are unruly, you can still be thankful for the fact that the school is open. At the very least, as long as your children are at school, you can go to work with an easy mind. Surely that is something to be thankful for. It is a good idea to lower your expectations somewhat, and focus on areas you have not previously been aware of, finding happiness there.

Relieving stress is one of the roles of the family so it is necessary to change your perspective slightly and experience new things in order to have a fresh outlook. If you look for activities that do not cost much and try these, you may well find it constructive.

Restrain desire and return to the basics

School bullies sometimes act the way they do as a result of stress in the home. Even in the case of fathers who mistreat their children, there is some reason for their violence. The same is true of mothers. In one sense, everyone is suffering at this time, so it is important to restrain desire and return to the basics. This will stop the violence.

When people marry, they are happy despite the fact they may have nothing. It is important to return to that kind of mindset, to lower your expectations and give thanks for everything that you have. At the root of most suffering lies desire. People tend to imagine that if things had continued as they were, they would have had much more; however, because their expectations have not been realized, they suffer.

If you return to the basics of Buddhism, you will realize that essentially there is no need for you to have the desires you now possess. You can live happily without holding onto these desires. This is a worthwhile attitude to aim for. If, on the other hand, your company has been restructured, resulting in your becoming busier, I recommend that you study and improve your work skills. The management seminars held at our organization will help you gain wisdom in the field of management.

3. How to Recover from a Divorce

Question: *I have been through a divorce and I am currently not in a relationship. I have heard that before we are born into this world, we plan the course our lives will take, but do these plans include divorce? I would like to remarry, but what is necessary in order to do this?*

Marriage and divorce are one's own responsibility

To start with your question about whether people include divorce in their life plan before they are born in this world, some people actually do. In these cases, there is a particular objective in including divorce in the plans. For instance, a divorce may be instrumental in leading someone to awaken to the Truth. When everything in life is going smoothly, when you are quite happy with the way things are, it can be very difficult to awaken to the Truth. However, bankruptcy, illness, divorce, the death of a loved one, or a prolonged or unusual illness of a family member may provide the necessary impetus. So someone who has an important mission conveying the Truth may plan to experience one or two major setbacks in their life in order that their heart will turn toward the Truth.

Conversely, although a person may not have planned to get divorced, their marriage may break down anyway. Today, this is very common. Decisions in this world are basically left to the free will of the individual, and once a person makes up his or her mind firmly about something, even the person's guardian spirit cannot change this decision. This is one of the laws of life.

The way in which a person lives their life here on Earth will determine where they go in the next world. This being the case, if it were not for a person's own free will, their fate would be governed solely by the skills of their guardian and guiding spirits, and life would not make any sense. What it boils down to is the principle of self-responsibility, meaning that marriage and divorce are ultimately determined by the free will of each individual. If a decision turns out badly, then it is the responsibility of that individual; the individual must pay the price.

**Reflect carefully on your thoughts and deeds,
and pray for your partner's happiness**

It is a fact that people who experience a divorce have not yet overcome their karma of relationships with the opposite sex and it is quite likely that they have created numerous problems in past incarnations. To overcome this kind of karma, it is first necessary to look at your past thoughts and actions up to the point when you divorced, seeing the divorce as an opportunity to practice self-reflection. It is most important that you reflect on things that happened as a result of your own improprieties in areas where you had some influence. This will take you forward another step.

Next you will need to get rid of any hatred toward your ex-partner. Forgive him or her and pray for that person's happiness in his or her new life. As long as there is hatred in your heart toward your ex-partner, the path to a bright future will never open up for you. Moreover, your strong feelings of ill-will could work to obstruct your ex-partner's remarriage. You may feel that as he or she has made you unhappy, your ex-partner has no right to happiness in the future, but what happens in this world cannot be divided simply into good and evil. Although both people in a marriage may be essentially good-hearted, the combination may result in unhappiness. Someone who was not able to establish a happy marriage with you might do well and find happiness with another. If your "ex" succeeds in this, he or she will be comforted, so please pray for his or her happiness.

What is necessary for remarriage

Finally, you ask what is necessary for you to remarry, and the answer to this is, as I said earlier, that first you need to reflect on your past. Then, if your guardian spirit feels that you will be able to carry out your mission on Earth better by remarrying, your guardian spirit will introduce you to your next partner.

In the heavenly world before we are born into this world, most people make a promise to marry a certain person who is their first choice. In most cases, however, there are four or five more people on Earth whose destiny may possibly be to marry you and they are even ranked in order from A to E. If one of these people remains unmarried, then your guardian spirit will swiftly arrange for the two of you to move into the same orbit. Although you may not be destined to marry anyone, there are some who have studied the Truth with you or worked with you in previous lives, and with the assistance of the heavenly world, this kind of spiritual bond may develop into a marriage relationship. As a result you will marry, even though you had not promised yourselves to one another before birth. Such cases are not rare.

What is important is that you refine the inner self, become filled with light, and live your life in hope. If you emanate light, people will be drawn to you and there will be every possibility of your remarrying. After this, leave everything to your guardian spirit. If you set a time limit and decide that you want to marry within one year, or six months, or three months, then it will become an attachment and cause you pain. In order to avoid this, just ask your guardian spirit to arrange for an appropriate partner to appear at the appropriate time, and then continue to refine yourself spiritually while you wait.

You do not need to blame yourself too much; just do whatever needs to be done and wait. Soon, the opportunity will present itself and you will meet someone who you realize is the one for you. When this happens, please act in a positive and constructive manner. The courage to make decisions is a virtue for both men and women. I am on your side to encourage you on your journey.

4. How to Avoid the Danger of Divorce Later in Life

Question: *Recently there has been a rise in the divorce rate among older couples once their children have grown up and left the home. Please tell me what should be done to avoid the danger of divorce in later life.*

Divorce among middle-aged couples is common where a husband has devoted himself to his job

In most cases divorce among middle-aged couples generally appears to be the decision of the woman. The husband has been devoted to his job and has come home late; he was happy with a simple dinner, while for breakfast he would just have a slice of toast before hurrying out again. What happens when a man like this, who has been so devoted to his work that he does not even bother to eat proper meals, retires and is left hanging around the house every day?

In most cases, it will create stress for his wife. When a man who was never seen in the home during the day retires and is left to mope around the house, his presence quickly becomes something his wife would rather do without.

Devoting all of one's attention to the children is not advisable

Another problem arises when a wife devotes one hundred percent of her attention to her children, looking to her husband only to bring home a monthly paycheck. When the children grow up and leave home, the couple will lose the only thing that held them together.

What should be done to avoid this? Raising children takes a lot of effort, but if you devote your attention to your children a hundred percent of the time, you will create problems for yourself later. Children must not become everything to their parents. When a woman is married, she is usually one hundred percent devoted to her husband, but this gradually changes when the first child is born. The amount of energy that she devotes to this child decides the future balance of attention between her husband and her children.

When the share of attention given to a child is exceptionally large, it may be because the child is difficult to raise or a woman finds motherhood taxing; either way this can result in her no longer giving enough attention to her husband. The number of children she has will also contribute to the amount of time she spends on them. It is only natural in raising children that the amount of energy she has to spend on them will increase, but at a certain point she has to draw a line. To devote oneself one hundred percent to one's children is too much.

Increasing contact between a couple

To avoid divorce in later life and to allow a couple to live happily together into old age, it is necessary that a wife does not devote one hundred percent of her energies to her children but leaves a share for her husband too. If she has given her children one hundred percent of her time and her husband none of it for most of their married life, when she has finished raising them and is suddenly faced with devoting herself one hundred percent to her husband, she may well feel it is too much for her.

So, in preparation for a return to the situation that existed before the children were born, when she gave one hundred percent to her husband, she needs to maintain a healthy balance. For example, she could set aside one day of the week when she joins her husband for something of mutual interest, thereby creating an opportunity for communication between them.

If a husband expends all his energy on his career, then there is a good chance of him divorcing when he is older. To avoid this, he should set aside time every week when he can talk with his wife, purposely making time for them to be together. As the children gradually require less attention, the couple can make the effort to increase the time they spend together. In this way they will have to adjust gradually to the coming situation, avoiding a sudden change in the amount of attention they give to one another.

Start early to find a purpose in life after retirement

In many cases where couples divorce in later life, the husband has devoted his entire life to his career and once that is taken away from him he has nothing left. If he is nothing without his job, this will be a problem. He should start early to create something that will give him a reason to live in old age.

Once you reach the age of fifty, it is time to start thinking about what you will do when you reach sixty. You need to ask yourself beforehand what you will do once you retire from work, and start investing in the study of something that will give your life some purpose in old age. Think of something you will want to do once you are older. People who are devoted to something that gives their life meaning radiate a brilliant light.

Planning for old age

Of course, there are couples where the wife goes out to work while the husband stays at home and they are probably as prone to dissatisfaction in old age as any other couple. Whatever the situation, to avoid divorce in old age it is necessary to think strategically in the way that I have set out here.

Do not devote one hundred percent of your attention to your children; as they grow up and require less care, take the opportunity to strengthen your relationship with your partner. To do this, set aside time to talk together, start early to plant and nurture the seeds for later life of an interest which will take the place of work and give meaning to your old age. It will be good for the two of you to share a similar interest. If you do not, you might find life together becomes hard as you get older. To sum up, planning for your old age is very important.

Chapter Three

Your Children

1. How to Raise Gifted Children

Question: *Recently, we have been hearing a lot about the importance of special education for young children while they are still infants, in connection with the fact that by the age of three, eighty percent of the human brain is already formed. My child is now eighteen months old and I am concerned about how to raise him. Is there something I should be doing to help him become a gifted child?*

Parents must learn to enjoy study

At eighteen months, a child is still virtually incapable of learning through its own efforts, but the child's brain is in the process of developing according to the tendencies of the soul. For this reason, determining the direction in which the soul is leading the development of the brain is of vital importance.

If your child is still eighteen months old, it may be a little early, but the best way of nurturing the intelligence of a child is for parents to demonstrate an enthusiasm for study themselves. Most parents will probably be disappointed to hear this, but it is the truth. Infants are too young to be taught in a formal way, but they learn a great deal through observing adults. The only people available for a baby to learn from are its parents and it is constantly watching their behavior. It is very observant, noticing all their habits and tendencies, the way they speak and even the way they think.

So, even if parents want their child to be a genius, if they themselves use abusive language and live in a slovenly way this will be unlikely. In this sort of situation, there is very little chance a child will turn out a genius. Occasionally, however, a brilliant soul from the heavenly world purposely chooses to be born into this kind of environment so that its outstanding quality will be highlighted; cases like this, however, are the exception. Basically, if you would like your child to grow up to be of above average intelligence, the most effective way is to let your child see your enthusiasm for study while he or she is still open and accepting.

The importance of nurturing positive mental attitudes in the home

Once a child enters primary school, school becomes the main influence, so the period prior to this is of great importance. A child's emotional base is formed from the age of two or three until about six. Emotions can be described as the expression of a person's thought tendencies. The formation of the emotions is extremely important. It is the emotions that decide whether a person will have a tendency to seek lofty and exalted ideals, or veer in the direction of brutality and cold-blooded cruelty, or any of the myriad personality types in between.

A child's emotional base is established by about the age of six, and it is possible to create spiritual leanings toward noble and lofty ideals before that age. I cannot emphasize enough the importance of this emotional education, and it is the influence of the parents that determines how the children turn out. For this reason, it is necessary that at least one of the parents demonstrates a love of study. If neither parent is capable of this, then it will be necessary to call in the assistance of a grandparent or someone else, just so long as there is someone in the house who likes to study.

If there is a grandparent who has been involved in intellectual pursuits and continued with these after retirement, it can have a powerful influence on a child. When a child is young, it is not unusual for both parents to be busy and unable to find much time for study. If this is the case in your home, look around to see whether there is an intellectual grandparent; if so, invite that person to your home occasionally. If there is no one like this close to you, there will be no alternative but for one of you to make a point of studying when you are in the presence of your child.

If this continues while the child is between the ages of about two and six years old, although they do not understand what is happening, children will quite naturally develop a liking for the atmosphere of study. This is an influence that will stay with a child for the rest of his or her life. If, on the other hand, during this period the parents abuse each other, displaying violent tendencies or exhibiting cruelty to living things, the child's mind will gradually become distorted. During this period, exposing the child to role models is vital. In bringing up a child, do not be easily swayed by the current trends.

Children look for role models

Children first start to understand their environment and exercise their own judgment from the age of about ten or eleven. It is at this age that a child begins to develop certain attitudes as a result of his or her own thoughts. Consequently, the best time to start appealing to a child's powers of reason in order to change patterns of behavior is from about ten or eleven. Up until this time, the main factor in shaping a child's character is the influence of the parents.

Between the ages of seven and eleven, a child's teachers as well as friends exert a powerful influence. Therefore, the question of whether or not children come into contact with good teachers is extremely important. This means that if they are not blessed with a good teacher at school, a substitute must be found to take the teacher's place. If there is no one suitable among your relatives, a university or high school student living in the neighborhood may serve your purpose. It would be good to invite a student who enjoys studying and is well brought up to your house occasionally to expose your child to this sort of role model.

It is important that there is someone close at hand who will exert a positive influence. Ideally it should be someone in whom children can see themselves in ten years time. This method of education is most important for children between the ages of seven and eleven. At this age, they search eagerly for people who can provide examples that they can follow. If there is no one for them to emulate, it will delay their development considerably; so it is important for parents to try to find someone who can serve as a role model.

If you can sow in children the seeds of a tendency to strive for ideals while they are still young, as they grow older this will flower naturally. For instance, if a child's parents like to read and there are a considerable number of books in the house, there is an eighty or ninety percent likelihood that the child will also become an avid reader. If, on the other hand, despite the fact he himself only subscribes to magazines, a father tells his children that they should enjoy reading, his efforts are unlikely to meet with success. While it is possible for children to develop a liking for reading as a result of their own efforts after they reach adulthood, if they are brought up in an environment where reading is a part of everyday life, they will learn to enjoy reading quite naturally. This demonstrates the importance of creating a stimulating environment for children.

Finally, I would like to add that while children are still in kindergarten or primary school it is important to teach them to carry out the tasks they are given properly and ensure that they learn the three "Rs"—reading, writing and arithmetic—to create a foundation for future studies. The appropriate time for starting to build more knowledge is the fourth year of elementary school.

2. A Method of Developing a Child's Gifts

Question: *What should a parent keep in mind in order to recognize and cultivate a child's natural gifts and abilities?*

Guide children and nurture their gifts

There are many different ways of raising children, depending on the child's character. However, speaking generally, one point that every parent needs to be aware of is the tendency of parents to look upon their children as possessions. Surprisingly, this is something that most parents do not realize they are doing.

It is easy for parents to fall into the trap of believing that they create their children themselves, and although this may be true of the body, the soul is something that already existed in the Real World before the child was born. Parents and children have their own individual character. So, bearing in mind that children will not necessarily follow their parents' wishes, it is important to raise them in a way that conforms to the child's innate spiritual nature and tendencies.

The parents must not try to dictate a child's future, saying: "He will take over as head of the family," "He will continue the family business," "He will become a doctor, a scholar, an artist," etc. Parents often hope that their children will manage to achieve what they themselves have failed to achieve, but in most cases, there is very little chance of the child succeeding where the parents have failed. If the father says, "I could not manage to do this, so now I am counting on you," it will only put immense pressure on the child.

As a child grows, the parents must discern the nature of the child's soul. Between the ages of ten and twenty, a child's gifts begin to reveal themselves and it is possible to tell whether a child is cut out for business, academia, or a career as a technician or a civil servant. If the aptitudes of a child are not evident by the time he or she is twelve, it simply means that it will take a little longer for the potential to become clear, and if this is the case, a child should be given a general education.

If, however, the gifts are already clear, then children should be led in the direction that will allow them to make the most of their abilities. The ultimate education is to believe in the power of the individual soul and allow a child to develop to the fullest in the direction in which he or she wants to grow.

A child does not need to experience the same hardships as parents

Next I would like to discuss the issue of personal values. The values that we learn to believe in can be divided into two types: values that are universally held, by other people as well as ourselves, and individual values that result from our own unique environment. Unless you can distinguish between these two kinds of values, mistakes can result.

Suppose a man has been brought up in a harsh environment deep in the mountains, but later comes to a big city, and after much hardship, succeeds in business. When he eventually comes to have children of his own, it is only natural that his children will lead a more privileged life than he did. On seeing this, the father may think, "They take their lifestyle for granted, they have no idea of how hard I struggled," and set about making his children experience the same hardships that he himself went through in his youth. This, however, is something that should be avoided.

Children are born in a different era from their parents and they have been brought up in a different environment; the parents should recognize this and raise their children differently. It is wrong to want them to suffer the same hardships you suffered, or to make them start from the same place as you did. Children start out from the environment created by their parents so it is only natural that they will go further than the parents, and this is something that parents must accept. Children stand on their parents' shoulders; their starting point is different. This means that parents should actually be proud and happy about the fact that their children progress beyond them.

To raise an angel of light

I would now like to talk about how to raise a child who is an angel of light, born from one of the realms of high spirits. Angels of light are entrusted with a mission to convey the Truth to others, to save people and lead them to happiness. For this reason, it is vital for an angel of light to attain a deep understanding of people. While still in primary or junior high school, they should read many classics and as much literature as possible that touches the soul.

The minds of these sorts of people need to be nourished.

Although they are born with great potential, this cannot be fulfilled unless they receive sufficient nourishment for their souls, otherwise they will not flourish and their development will be delayed. Parents and grandparents who study and practice the Truth in their daily lives will naturally provide an ideal environment in which children can develop their true potential for the future.

In China there is a saying, "Virtue exists in a house which has smelled of books for one hundred years." What this means is that if the parents read a lot, it will be easy for children to adopt the same lifestyle. For instance, Japanese physicist Hideki Yukawa (1907–1981)[1] was born into a family in which there were many scholars, and this provided him with a domestic environment ideal for his studies.

It is also necessary for angels of light to be taught what other angels have achieved in the past.[2] This will become the foundation from which they can take the next step, so they should be encouraged to study the words and writings of great figures of the past. This will serve as a grounding, allowing them to achieve great things once they become members of society.

Whether or not people have been educated in this way up to the age of twenty will make a huge difference later in their lives. I cannot stress too much the importance of this. If these children are encouraged while still young to read the words and writings of the angels who preceded them, their development will be straightfor-

---

[1] Hideki Yukawa was a physicist who proposed a new theory of nuclear forces and predicted the existence of the meson. He was awarded the Nobel Prize for Physics in 1949 for research into the theory of elementary particles.

[2] Refer to *The Golden Laws* by Ryuho Okawa..

ward and they will follow a right path. This is how angels of light should be educated.

Before I finish this section, I would like to touch on the subject of the importance of play. There may be parents who are enthusiastic supporters of study, but they should not forget that while children are still in kindergarten, primary or junior high school, play serves to assist a child's overall intellectual development, providing numerous experiences that are impossible to gain through study alone. Play can teach a child the importance of keeping promises, the roles of leader and follower, and develop creativity.

3. Parents Should Work with Their Children to Prevent Delinquency and Absence from School

Question: *I have a daughter who is in the fourth year of primary school. She is violent at home and is repeatedly absent from school. Is there any effective means of preventing this?*

Parents must first rebuild their own lives
When a child is violent at home and refuses to go to school for long periods, it is highly likely that the family is being affected by negative spiritual influences. Moreover, if a child is still young, the cause of his or her misbehavior also lies with the parents. Although parents may struggle to find some way of curing their child, the same kind of spiritual influences that affect the child are generally influencing them as well, so a kind of spiritual battle is taking place within the family. If a child is still young, the parents should begin by determining to change their own way of life, otherwise it will prove impossible for them to find a solution.

Strangely enough, this kind of problem is most common in

households where the parents are held in high regard in society and exert a lot of influence through their jobs. If the parents are bearing a load that exceeds their own capabilities, this distortion will often manifest itself through the children.

The weakest person in the family will most likely be the target of negative spiritual influences, and manifest problems. For instance, if the parents are difficult targets, the spirits exerting a negative influence will attack the children. These spirits always look for the weakest targets.

The only way to prevent this is to focus on strengthening your inner light. If the parents' inner light is strong, the negative influences cast over the children will be weakened and the children will quickly recover. The most effective measure for increasing this light is for the parents to study the Truth. Then, the parents should be resolute so that the entire family can join forces to try to overcome the problem. Of special importance is exploring the Right Mind as taught by Happy Science. There is obviously some mistake in the minds of the family members, so it is necessary for every member of the family to try to practice the exploration of the Right Mind.

Children rebel against being made to feel guilty

Children raised in the homes of upright people who have a strong awareness of sin, who are strict and judgmental, and subconsciously guide their children to feel guilty, will often rebel. In these cases, the problem is more basic than that of spiritual influences—the children's souls are rebelling against the sense of guilt that is being imposed on them by their parents. The children resent being bound by the will of their parents, and having their parents impose their own values on them.

The children notice the inconsistency in their parents' attitudes, and think that although they pretend to be good and put on airs when they are with others, they are really not half of what they pretend to be. They feel it is unfair to have feelings of guilt forced upon them. When this happens, rebellion wells up in their hearts, which triggers some spiritual influence.

This type of parent needs to learn that physically, although they may be parent and child, their souls are different. They have to learn to loosen the bonds with which they try to bind their children, attempting to make them act as they would like. So, trust your children and resist interfering too much. Although spiritual influences come into it to some extent, in most cases it is the parents' attitude to their children that lies at the root of the problem. It is the result of parents interfering too much in their children's lives.

Do not fall into the trap of giving false love

Often when parents interfere in their children's lives they do so out of a subconscious desire to reduce their own stress. They vent feelings on their children that they cannot express outside the home. For instance, there are parents who say, "I work very hard so that you can have everything," when in fact what they are really doing is taking out their frustrations on their children. The parents need to practice self-reflection and ask themselves whether they are using their children as a means of relieving the stress they themselves are experiencing.

Although they may believe that they are giving love, the parents are actually binding their children to try to make them be the way they would like, exercising a false love that is like glue. They have a strong desire to control everything, and as a result, they try to lock their children in "cages" like birds. This is not a true form of "love that gives" but actually "love that takes." As their children gradually grow to adulthood and independence, the parents should look upon them with joy in their hearts, but some think of their children as "toys." There are more than a few adults who, although splendid people in their own right, think of their children as being there simply for their own amusement.

There are, for instance, parents who lament, "I am always telling you to get married, but you show no sign of interest," when in fact they are the ones who are preventing marriage. The truth is that they do not want to let their child go, so they say all kinds of things to bind their offspring to them, and what is more, they are not even aware of what they are doing. In this way, numerous forms of false love, in what at first glance appears to be "love that gives," develop in the relationship between parent and child. It is important that you recognize what you are actually doing.

To return to the domestic violence and absence from school that you mention in your question: As a mother, remember not to speak badly of your husband to your children, and not to blame him for his faults while ignoring your own shortcomings. Harmony between a husband and wife has a powerful influence on children. Respect for one another and a balance in taking initiative in the home are very important.

4. For Children with Physical Disabilities

Question: *Please give some advice to children who are physically disabled and to their parents.*

Different experiences expedite the soul's learning

A person's life is not limited to the life they are living now in this physical world; everyone experiences numerous incarnations. Moreover, when we are born, we do not always necessarily select a smooth life, because if we did, it would not contribute much to the soul's learning. For this reason we sometimes elect to undergo extreme experiences.

Among their numerous incarnations, people are generally born at least once with some kind of physical disability. In order to realize how fortunate it is to inhabit a healthy body, people are born into an environment where they suffer some sort of disability. This is something that everyone will experience and naturally some people are now at that stage.

Of course, there are times when a disability has not been planned as a form of spiritual refinement, but has occurred later in life as the result of an accident or illness. However, a person's life plan is not necessarily completely fixed; there are various possibilities for change and people will live their lives within a range of possibilities.

Do not use your disability as an excuse

The basic rule for people who suffer some kind of disability is that they should not use it as an excuse. Even though they are disabled, it is important that they live in such a way as to turn the situation into something positive. If they live their lives simply using their disability as an excuse, it will never be of benefit to them. This is an undeniable fact.

So, if you meet a disabled child, please tell them that they have been chosen to lead a wonderful life. Although they may start out at a disadvantage, they can have a wonderful life by using their adverse circumstances as a springboard to get ahead and open up a path before them.

The American philosopher, Dale Carnegie (1888–1955), was famous for books such as *How to Stop Worrying and Start Living* and *How to Win Friends and Influence People*. When playing as a child, he jumped out of a window but the ring he was wearing caught on a nail, and he lost the index finger of his left hand. However, in later years, he referred to this saying, "I never worried about the loss of my finger. I realized that I was missing a finger no more than once a month." He worked so positively and energetically throughout his life that most of the time he forgot that his finger was missing.

If you suffer some kind of disability, there is no point in worrying about it to the exclusion of all else. If you focus your energies on living in a positive way you will find that in the end, your life will have been enriched as a result. People are incapable of thinking of two things at the same time. You can take advantage of this truth by always thinking about the good that will come out of any experience.

The distance you have traveled from the starting line will be measured

Although your child may have some kind of disability, do not give in to despair. Please tell children that it is precisely because they have a disability that they will be able to achieve all the more. Life has many different aspects and a handicap need not necessarily be a reason for unhappiness.

The fact that people all start from different points is, to a certain extent, unavoidable. However, although the starting lines may differ, we will all be judged according to our progress and the amount of effort we have made. Someone who is born into a wealthy family, who has good health and a sharp mind, will be measured according to how far he or she has managed to move forward from this starting point. Others may start out with the most unfavorable circumstances and they will be judged according to the progress they have made from *their* starting line.

Whatever the case, the distance your soul has traveled is what is important; you will look back over your life and say, "I managed to walk this far," "I managed to run this far." If you look at the situation in this way, I believe you will be able to overcome the difficulties you face. There may be hard times, but it is in such circumstances that you should look on the bright side and think positively.

I would like to finish by reminding you that although people may have a physical disability, there is nothing wrong with their soul. When people with disabilities return to the Real World after they die, they will find themselves completely free, and some will awaken to the true meaning of their life as a workbook of problems to be solved.

5. How to Deal with Children Addicted to Video Games

Question: *My son, at present in the second year of junior high school, has been enthralled by video games since he was in primary school. He claims that video games help reduce stress, but I have heard that they blunt the intellect and are an impediment to study, so I am worried about their effect on his development. How should I deal with the situation?*

Leave him to his own devices for a while

The way in which this should be dealt with depends on how you want your son to turn out in the future. Parents who want their children to excel in society tend to be too strict or to nag, but if you are happy to let your son grow in his own way, you probably do not have to worry too much about it. The measures that parents take will differ from family to family.

With regard to the video games themselves, it is a fact that they are very popular and children who do not play them may find themselves left out of conversations with their peers at school. However, the games tire the eyes and the brain, and so they become an obstacle to study.

There are probably very few adults who would consider playing video games at this juncture in their lives, and even if they did, they would not do it very well, inducing a sense of inferiority. However, children excel at these games, showing that they are riding the wave of the future. It is necessary to recognize that these games represent the coming of a new era.

Although children may become engrossed in video games, if they have any other talents, these will manifest in some way. Talent is like a tulip bulb—when the right time comes, it will send out shoots. From the buds of a yellow tulip, a yellow flower will bloom, and from the buds of a red tulip, a red flower. So if you think that it is still too early for your child's gifts to develop, it is important that you leave him to his own devices for a while and watch calmly from a distance to see what kind of buds come forth.

When observing your son it is vital to remember that, as I said, although you are parent and child, your souls are different. A parent is not free to mold a child as he or she sees fit. The child knows very well what kind of soul he or she is. What kind of bulb your child is will be quite obvious when the shoots appear and the flowers bloom, so you just have to wait a bit longer. It is inevitable that a child will do what is popular among his peers before true individuality manifests itself.

Set an age limit for video games

What is important is the way in which you view your child's gifts. If you believe that your son will grow up to work in the video game industry, then there is no problem, but if you think that he is the type of child who needs to devote himself to his studies to open up a path to success, perhaps you should consider putting an age limit on his playing. For example, you could say that it is all right for him to play video games while he is in junior high school, but that he must give them up once he enters senior high. If you do this, although you are family, it will be as though you have made a contract. By allowing him to play for a certain period, your son will feel the need to fulfill your expectations.

This technique is not limited to video games, but can also be used with children who are avid readers of comic books. For instance if children become hooked on comics in the first year of junior high school, you can tell them that it is all right to read comics until their third year, but once they enter senior high school they must stop. There again, if they start reading comics in primary school, you can say that it is all right for them to continue until they graduate but after that they must stop. In this way, by giving them the freedom to read what they like for two or three years, they will remember what you have said.

If you suddenly forbid a child from doing something that they find absorbing, they will immediately start doing something else in reaction. On the other hand, if you say "you may do it now, but you will have to stop later," not banning it outright, you will avoid making them rebel against your wishes. It is important that you teach children the right time to make changes in their lives. If children show promise in academic studies, it may be a good idea to decide how much time they should be allowed to play video games each day, and advise them to make a schedule and plan how long they will spend studying.

The last resort is just to accept the situation. Regardless of what sort of flower it is, a child's gifts will reveal themselves when the time is right. It is impossible for a cherry blossom to bloom from a tulip, so, in the final analysis, trust your child's abilities. It is important to realize that parents can only provide the water and fertilizer, while the praise of society will act like the sun; you cannot force a flower to bloom. No matter how hard a child's parents may try, they will not be able to change the type of flower that will blossom.

To sum up, your best course of action is to set a deadline, to say that your son is allowed to do something until he reaches a certain age but after that he has to stop. This is my advice to you. Of course, it may be that your son has a special talent for games and computers. Computer viruses that destroy computer programs are becoming an international problem and anti-virus programs are highly sought after. There was a Japanese high school student who developed one such program that was so successful he was able to start his own company. This grew rapidly and received a lot of inquiries from overseas companies. It is difficult to jump to conclusions about what is good and what is bad, so it is better to give children the space to develop their own potential.

6. Religious Education to Encourage a Right Way of Living

Question: *I would like to teach my children the right way to live from an early age. At what age should I begin teaching self-reflection, meditation and prayer? As a parent, what should I keep in mind when offering this sort of spiritual guidance?*

Self-reflection can be taught from the age of one

While people can, to a certain extent, start to practice meditation from the age of about fifteen, this may be a little too difficult for younger children. Of self-reflection, meditation and prayer, self-reflection can be started the earliest. If it is taught properly, a child can practice self-reflection from the age of one. Although they are not yet able to pray, children of one or two years of age can start self-reflection.

It is possible to start teaching very young children the difference between right and wrong clearly in simple issues, and instructing them to say "sorry" when they do something wrong. That is all you can do in the beginning. As they get older they will be able to understand more complicated self-reflection, but while they are still young the first step is to have them apologize on the spot as soon as they have done something wrong. At about three years old, they should be able to reflect on themselves and their actions more clearly, and by the time they start primary school they will be able to do this properly.

Of course, when teaching a child to practice self-reflection, it is important that the parents themselves do it. If you are not capable of self-reflection yourself, you cannot expect your child to do it. First of all, the parents must live in such a way that they have no problem with their children emulating them.

Give thanks every day in prayer

Prayer can also be started at a relatively early age. If you wait until a child is three or four years old, that should be old enough. Prayers should be said at set times every day, such as before breakfast, before dinner, or before going to bed. You can teach children to put their hands together in prayer, but if they are too young for this, you do not have to stick to this.

Start with a prayer of gratitude, because even a small child can manage this. In the morning, the children can offer a simple prayer such as: "Thank you for giving me this day. I will live this day to the fullest." It is good if the child makes some kind of promise like this in the prayer. Before the evening meal, the prayer can include self-reflection, for instance: "Thank you for giving me good health today. I have learned a lot." This is a prayer of gratitude that includes the elements of self-reflection. This will be sufficient while the child is still young.

Nurture a loving heart and the desire to help others

When children reach the age of about twelve they will be able to practice self-reflection and prayer in a more precise way, following the Truth more closely. They can read and understand books of the Truth and so are able to reflect on their thoughts and deeds for themselves.

When they pray, I would like their prayers to be positive and constructive. Eventually they will go out into society on their own, so the ideal would be for them to pray to be of service to the world. If they continue doing this for between three and six years while they are still teenagers, they will definitely turn out to be useful members of society.

If children harbor the desire to be of use to the world, they will study for the sake of other people, rather than for selfish ends or simply to compete with others. Then they will find love growing in their hearts. A loving heart is what is most important. Parents should teach their children to nurture a loving heart while they are still at school. To do this, parents need to explain that we are all children of God, able to live because of the efforts of so many other people, and that when we grow up we must give something back to society.

If you have managed to instill the desire to be of service to others into your child by the time he or she reaches the age of eighteen, then you can consider yourself to have been successful as a parent. This is the minimum requirement to be a good parent. There are many other difficult subjects that have to be dealt with, but first I would like you to concentrate on achieving this.

Are you able to explain your outlook on life simply?

The books of the Truth are written in simple language; however, in many cases, it is difficult even for adults to practice the teachings they contain. I would like all parents to read books of Truth and understand them thoroughly.

When you return to the other world, the question of whether or not you have been able to achieve the most basic level of enlightenment will depend on your ability to explain your own enlightenment simply, in a way that even children can understand. Even if you have studied a great deal of abstract philosophy, unless you are able to explain your own enlightenment and your own views on life in simple terms that even children can understand, then you have not really understood the Truth and will find it difficult to pass through the gates of heaven.

7. Religious Education Is Needed to Prevent Delinquency

Question: *Juvenile delinquency and crime are now on the increase and the average age of offenders is dropping. What will happen to the souls of* *these young people if they are unfortunate enough to die young without having learned about the other world or repented their deeds?*

What happens after death

Although all juvenile offenders are young, their age varies—so it is difficult to generalize. Children start to become aware of the world and exercise their own judgment at the age of about ten or eleven, and those who meet with unhappy deaths before this time will find it difficult to return to the other world. In most cases, they remain near their parents. As a result, unless the parents relieve the pain of the children and help them to return to heaven, they will remain with the parents until the parents die so that they can travel together to the other world.

Once children become aware of the outside world, they start to become responsible for their own actions. So teenagers whose behavior is delinquent or who commit crimes will have to take responsibility for the consequences of their own behavior, according to the law of cause and effect. As a result, if they die before becoming aware of their mistakes and repenting, they cannot escape going to hell.[3]

The hell realm encompasses a variety of regions, but those to which young people go are limited in number. There is one area at a relatively shallow level that is inhabited by those who have inflicted injury, used violence, or threatened others; it is like an underworld of gangsters and this is where most of these young

---

[3] Hell is a training ground where those who have led a life of wrongdoing will go after death to reflect their thoughts and deeds while living on Earth. However, they have chances to return to heaven and start a new life through self-reflection and repentance. For more precise descriptions of hell, please refer to Chapter 1 of *The Laws of Eternity* by Ryuho Okawa.

people will go. There are other places where those guilty of sex crimes go, while those who have committed numerous thefts will find themselves in the Hell of Beasts.

In the majority of cases, juvenile delinquency occurs as a result of emotional disturbance, generally expressing itself in domestic violence, or fights with peers. The hearts of these young people are in tune with the Ashura Realm,[4] that is to say, the Hell of Strife. This is a place of constant fear where the inhabitants feel they must beat others or be beaten themselves. To be quite blunt, it will be a very long time before any of them awaken to a right way of life.

Teaching faith in the home

It is safe to say that one cause of juvenile delinquency is a lack of education in the home or, to be more precise, a lack of religious education. This is the main problem. So, it is necessary to begin in the home by teaching faith. If at least one member of a family belongs to Happy Science, it will be helpful, because he or she can convey a knowledge of the Truth to the rest of the family.

The majority of juvenile crimes are the result of emotional disturbance due to the fact that a religious conscience has not been developed in the home. The fact that the parents lack a basic knowledge of religious truth is one major cause of this. These children could be saved if only the parents were to make the effort. However, because they do not bother, the children are left to go astray. So the first step is for parents to learn the Truth and pass it on to their children.

---

[4]   Ashura (*Asura* in Sanskrit) refers to the evil and fearsome spirits fond of fighting.

Chapter Four

Creating a Happier Family

1. Making the Home Happier

Question: *I live with my husband, our three children and my mother-in-law. My mother-in-law is a stingy woman whom I find difficult to love. My husband likes to gamble, and while I accept this, I find him difficult to respect. He is currently suffering from neuralgia on the left side of his body, which sometimes gives rise to severe headaches. The youngest of our children is a little disobedient. As a daughter-in-law, wife and mother, what kind of attitude should I adopt?*

A wife and mother-in-law learn from one another

In Asian countries in particular, there are many families where couples live with the parents of the husband or wife after they marry. When it comes to the relationship between a wife and a mother-in-law, we cannot overlook the fact that a rivalry exists between them. Men compete with each other in the workplace to prove who is most able, while women also possess certain intangible abilities and a wife and her mother-in-law compete to prove who is more capable. That is the reason the relationship between these two women is often not very good. Moreover, a wife and a mother-in-law belong to different generations and their ways of thinking are different, so this can also contribute to the problem.

Give the elderly hope for the next world

Generally speaking, elderly people tend to take love from others, and to a certain extent, this cannot be helped. It is unavoidable that the elderly progressively come to resemble young children, mostly as a result of the deterioration of bodily functions. The deterioration of the brain results in senility and an increase in selfishness. Eventually old people may become like three-year-old children, petulant, unwilling to listen to others, and acting on impulse.

Because they believe that they do not have much longer to live and they could die at any time, they feel they have to speak their mind and do everything they want while they still have the chance. They become impatient and end up doing things that appear odd to others. If, as they approach the end of their lives, they feel society has no further use for them, they lose confidence and hope for the future, trying to find something to give comfort to the heart.

When an older person behaves in an extremely selfish way, it is usually the result of some negative spiritual influence. Senility is not always solely due to the deterioration of the brain; in many cases it is caused by some spiritual disturbance. As people get older, their feelings of unease increase, and they begin to suffer more and more from a sense of persecution. If they constantly complain that their son or daughter-in-law does nothing for them, or that society does not acknowledge them, their discontent will grow and they will develop a mental attitude that attracts spirits from hell.

Once possession by these spirits has been eradicated and they have hope for the future, older people change quite remarkably. For this reason it is important that they possess a firm understanding of the next world. They must be taught that death is merely graduating from this world and there is nothing dreadful about it. When they leave this world they will be given a kind of "report card," and if they have good marks for behavior, they will not have any trouble. To finish one's spiritual refinement here on Earth and return to the other world is much the same as graduating from school to go on to the next level, starting work out in society. It is an extremely happy occasion.

The only people who need to fear the next world are those who will have to go to hell. If you have done your best to live your life according to the will of God, if you have carried out the mission entrusted to you in this world and completed your studies of the next world, and feel as though all you have to do now is wait for death, you can look forward to being called to the next world. Your heart will be filled with a sense of release.

How to grow old gracefully

In the course of our lives we pass through various phases, but old age is particularly important. Although you may be good at your job and have a good reputation while you are young, if you live in a negative way in your later years, you may find that after you leave this world a negative outcome awaits. For this reason, even when you are still young, you always need to be thinking of ways that will allow you to live out your old age in peace so that you will be able to grow old gracefully.

If you have a sound faith and have made a study of the next world, you should be able to grow old gracefully. If you have explored and studied the Truth for many years at Happy Science, when you approach death your gaze will always be peaceful and a smile never far from your lips. When you realize that your departure from this world is not far off, you will be able to speak kindly to those around you. When the end finally comes, you will draw your last breath quite naturally and set out for the next world. This is the happiest way to die. To be able to die without causing those nearest you any trouble is the best way to go.

Old age is the time to study how to make the transition to the next world as smooth as possible. For this reason, religious activities are particularly important for the elderly. The activities of Happy Science will, of course, greatly help people to die peacefully and return to heaven. I would like elderly people to study the books of Truth and the Happy Science Monthly magazine published by our organization. If their eyes are bad and they find it difficult to read, they can study using our cassette tapes, CDs or videos. If they study and understand the Truth well, they will be able to graduate from this world with full marks, making their transition to the next world smooth.

Do not become a "judge" in your home

Next is your concern about your husband. From what you have told me, I assume that he is somewhat spiritually disturbed. Among the various negative spiritual influences are the effects of animal spirits, and your husband seems to be under the influence of the spirit of a snake.[1] Those who are affected by a snake spirit feel great pressure in the head and suffer from very bad headaches. Snake spirits also often possess a victim's legs.

People who are under the influence of snake spirits are

---

[1]   The spirit world is a world of thought and the inhabitants take on a form that is an exact reflection of their thoughts. Those who have acquired animalistic tendencies while living on Earth will go to a hell known as the Hell of Beasts after they die. Those in hell try to escape their agony by possessing people on Earth whose thoughts are the same wavelength. If people come under negative spiritual influences, they are apt to become ill. Refer to Chapter 4 of *An Unshakable Mind* by Ryuho Okawa.

characteristically lacking a cheerful disposition and they always seem to have a load on their mind. People with a tendency to long-windedness and hesitation, whose minds are always filled with different thoughts and who are quick to pick on others' faults, are prone to possession by snake spirits. It is necessary for them to make an effort to be more light-hearted.

However, if you tell your husband this too persistently, it will cause him to resist, so it is better that you first try to change yourself. A husband and wife are like mirrors that reflect each other; if one undergoes a transformation, the other will also change.

With regard to your children, it is only natural for young people to go through a rebellious phase, so try to think of ways to keep the damage this causes to a minimum and even to create something positive out of it.

What you most need to keep at the forefront of your mind is not to judge your family. The ideal is that by your very presence, you are able to bring a breath of happiness to those around you. If you act like a judge, handing out verdicts on family members, it will only cause them to become even more obstructive. Rather than judging them, adopt a softer approach that will increase happiness in the family.

Eliminate any negative spiritual influences from the home

Smiles are always present in a household where all negative spiritual influences have been banished and which is under the protection of guardian spirits. However, once a home starts coming under the negative influences of stray spirits, you suddenly start noticing the faults of other family members, and complaints and dissatisfaction begin to grow. For instance, if a husband's guardian spirit is present, smiling beside him, his wife will seem very beautiful to him. If, on the other hand, his guardian spirit disappears and instead two or three stray spirits have some influence over him, he will find fault with everything his wife does, saying, "I don't like your hairstyle," "I don't like your clothes," "I don't like the way you laugh," or "Your cooking tastes bad." To be possessed by a stray spirit is like wearing tinted glasses, it only allows people to see the negative.

So if you find yourself always noticing others' faults, before you start criticizing them, it is important to realize that you have come under a negative spiritual influence and do something to stop it. The cassette tapes and CDs of my lectures provide an effective tool for driving out negative spiritual influences. As soon as you play one of these, stray spirits will flee. When you feel the approach of a stray spirit, it is a good idea to put on one of my cassettes or CDs. For instance, if you are working in the kitchen and feel strangely irritated, just play one of them as you work. In the same way, if you find it strangely difficult to get to sleep at night, play one. If you meet someone who is possessed by a stray spirit, it is possible the spirit may transfer itself to you, but if you play one of my tapes or CDs, it will drive the spirit away.

The videotapes of my lectures are even more powerful than the cassettes or CDs. Older people or young children who find reading difficult can benefit from watching my videos. For people who do not like to read, the videos are a good substitute. Reciting one of the basic sutras of Happy Science, *Buddha's Teaching: The Dharma of the Right Mind*, and our prayer books, *Prayers I* and *Prayers II*, is extremely effective. Reading one of my books will also have an effect; if you read through a chapter of one of my books on the Truth, light will pour into you and with that light stray spirits will be sent away. Of course, if you participate in one of the ritual prayer services for eliminating negative spiritual influences that are held at the temples and branches of our organization, this will have a tremendous effect.

Please banish all the negative spiritual influences from your household. If you do this, you will find that your home becomes much happier. If you continue striving to further refine yourself spiritually at our organization, I can guarantee that your household will become a Utopia.

2. The Secret of a Wonderful Old Age

Question: *What can be done to help the elderly? Also, what should the elderly bear in mind as they go about their daily lives?*

Speak positively

Elderly people all find themselves in different situations so it is difficult to generalize, but if I were asked for a single piece of advice I would offer the following: When dealing with the elderly, always speak positively. As people grow older, their bodies become weaker, leading them to become more pessimistic and prone to voicing complaints and dissatisfactions. Moreover, despite the fact that they have built up a large stock of experience in the course of their lives, their speech and behavior become increasingly childish. This is unavoidable.

They do not know how much longer they have to live, whether they have ten or twenty years more. What is important, however, is that they spend their remaining time on Earth truly happy. When considering the happiness of an older person and the people around him or her, there is a vast difference between ten years of complaint and dissatisfaction, of sadness and pain, as compared to ten years without any complaints at all. Complaining will not improve a situation. It is important that the elderly do not spend their days discontented and complaining, but have a positive attitude. To this end, a habit of taking suitable exercise will be of help.

Think of life as lasting one hundred and twenty years, spend your later years happily

What I should particularly like to say to my older readers is, as I also said in my book *Invincible Thinking*,[2] you should think of your life expectancy as being one hundred and twenty years. There are not many people who actually manage to live to the age of one hundred and twenty, but if you think that you will live that long, you will find that your complaints and discontent will disappear. So even if you die before you reach that age, at say, eighty or ninety, you will have been able to live a wonderful life.

As people get older, they are prone to say in a dissatisfied way that they do not have much longer to live, but this is not going to make their lives any better. It would be much better if they were to believe that they still had until they were one hundred and twenty, and lived accordingly. If they believed that they were going to live to one hundred and twenty, then most people would still have several decades to look forward to. For instance, if they are now sixty years old, it would mean that they have another sixty years left to them. Thinking in this way, they will realize that they still have plenty to do in life. They will say, "If I have another sixty years, there is no point in just complaining, I have a lot left to do.

---

[2]   Refer to Part 2, Section 9 of *Invincible Thinking* by Ryuho Okawa.

I must do this and I must do that . . ." and draw up a plan. This is an ideal way to live.

While living their lives to the fullest, one day they will be called back to the other world. When this happens, it is best that they are able to smile at those who have come to see them off and leave this world in a graceful, light-hearted way. This guarantees them happiness after they leave this world. Even if someone leads a wonderful life up to the age of forty or fifty, if they are miserable after that, things will not go well for them after they have died. It is important to enjoy a wonderful old age. To do this, it is important to plan for the future in a positive and constructive way, and the best way to achieve this is to believe that you are going to live to the age of one hundred and twenty, and act accordingly.

Theoretically speaking, the idea of living till the age of one hundred and twenty is not a lie. It is possible for people to lengthen the span of their years. The most common reason people leave this world is that there is no further reason for them to remain, their continued existence is not of vital significance. People who feel their lives do have significance are able to extend their time here if they so decide. However, most people finish their work when they are fifty or sixty years old, and having nothing left to do, are unable to live for another sixty years.

To avoid this, it is vitally important that you plan for a second or even a third career. Ideally, it should be something that will develop in a quite different way to what has come before. If you have worked as the president of a company until the age of seventy or eighty, be prepared to stand aside for your successor and begin a new life. In order to achieve this, it is necessary to start making preparations about ten years ahead and plan for a different kind of life. Once you have decided that you are going to start a certain sort of life from the age of seventy, begin preparing for it from around the time you are sixty. If you decide to start a new life from the age of eighty, then prepare for it from the age of seventy.

As you become involved in these preparations, you will find that you begin to think in a more constructive and positive fashion. You will find that you have so much to do that you will begrudge wasting any time. In this way, by taking a proactive approach you will find that you cannot afford to waste time complaining. This is an extremely happy situation to be in. An old age filled with light is the kind of life to aim for. This will bring happiness not only to you, but to those around you.

Give the elderly something to live for

To sum up what I have said so far, it is important to be as positive and constructive as possible when talking to the elderly. Tell them to think of their life as lasting one hundred and twenty years, and encourage them to live accordingly.

In addition, it is also necessary to offer older people something to live for. For an older person, life's purpose counts for everything; if they have something to live for, life will be rose-colored, but without a purpose, everything will appear gray. In fact, what is most important for elderly people is a purpose for living, so help your parents to find this. Without this purpose, even if you tell them to reflect on past thoughts and deeds, they will find it difficult.

When elderly people are fighting illness, their efforts should be focused on expressing peace through facial expressions, and offering love through their words. It is important that they always keep smiling and making an effort to speak calmly and lovingly. If they express their gratitude to those around to ease their labors, they will find that people treat them even better. Finally, tell older people to look forward to the enjoyable work that awaits them in heaven.

3. Diet and Control of the Mind

Question: *It is often said that illness stems from the mind. However, there are many people around me who have managed to overcome their illnesses by correcting imbalances in their diet. What are the effects of diet and of controlling the mind on health?*

The tendencies of the mind influence diet

Diet is not unrelated to the mind. For instance, when it comes to food, the origin of our likes and dislikes is the mind. An imbalanced mind often gives rise to dietary preferences and dislikes. People who are not fussy about what they eat will be magnanimous toward others and will be able to interact in a friendly way with virtually anyone. Conversely, people who are extremely fussy about what they eat will also be fussy when it comes to choosing friends.

So the mind also influences what we eat. Generally speaking, the tendencies of the mind manifest in our diet, this being true both at the individual and the group level. The standard diet in Western countries is rich in meat, and this is a manifestation of the fighting spirit of the people, whose souls tend to be aggressive. The opposite can be seen in many Eastern countries where the diet is largely vegetarian and the people are quiet and patient, leading quiet lives. In some Eastern countries, diet has been increasingly westernized in recent years, partly as a result of the way that people's attitudes have changed. In other words, not only people's diet but also their way of thinking and lifestyles have become west-ernized. As a result, people's bodies have adapted to their new diet.

Controlling the mind and improving diet

Approximately seventy percent of all illness is a result of spiritual phenomena, such as negative spiritual influences, and this is due to the state of mind of an individual. There are also many other factors that combine to create illness, such as lack of exercise, nutritional imbalances and work-induced stress.

If your question is asking whether it is possible for a person to improve their health not only through a person's state of mind but also through diet, then the answer is yes, and in a way it is a good method. Of course, it is best if you can govern your mind, but for those who have difficulty doing so, it is possible to treat illness through controlling your diet.

Sometimes the influence of a physical problem can be the cause of a mental problem. The majority of lifestyle-related diseases, for instance, fall into this category. However, people who suffer from high blood pressure or damage internal organs by overindulging in food, alcohol or fatty foods have only themselves to blame. People whose health has suffered as the result of a nutritional imbalance can recover by setting about improving their diet. This can bring about a healthy state of mind as well.

What it boils down to is that both the mind and diet are important for good health, the mind bearing about seventy percent of the responsibility. This is a basic fact. The influence of problems of the mind on health is more common. However, people who do not understand this should start by working on their diet. A good piece of advice is to eat a well-balanced diet to make yourself healthy again. Once people are fit and find it easier to keep a smile on their face, they will get on better with others and their minds will come back into harmony.

In most cases when it comes to the relationship between the mind and body, the mind is more important, but it is difficult to be specific. It is like the problem of chicken and egg; which comes first? It is impossible to offer a simple solution.

4. The Effect of the Brain and the Soul on the Intellect

Question: *Is a person's intellect governed by their soul, or is it dependent on physical factors as a result of the genes inherited from parents?*

Children are born as a result of the spiritual bond with parents

Parents and children have a deep spiritual connection. In most cases, a child is not born to a particular pair of parents by chance. There are occasions where a change in a situation has caused a child to be born to a parent with whom there has been no previous relationship. However, in the vast majority of cases a child is born to a particular parent as a result of their spiritual connection. The connection may relate to the father or the mother, but usually both.

In what situations is a child born to a particular parent or parents? There are three main factors that control who a child's parents will be. The most common is that they have been family members together in past lives, too. This accounts for about sixty to seventy percent of all births. Another common situation is when the child wants to inherit specific characteristics or skills from a parent in order to carry out a task on Earth. In this case, the child will be born into the necessary family environment. The third type of situation is when a guiding spirit decides to whom the child should be born. Of course, some kind of spiritual connection exists between the parent and child, but souls who are indecisive will be matched with suitable parents so that they can be born on Earth.

Looking at the second instance, in which a soul chooses parents according to their abilities and tendencies, we can say that highly developed souls have a strong tendency to select the most appropriate parents. However, there is a law that those of the same spiritual vibration attract one another, so to a certain extent souls will only be able to be born to parents who are of a similar spiritual wavelength. As a result there is a tendency for a talented soul to look for people of a similar spiritual wavelength who possess the appropriate talents to be their parents.

When people live in the world of souls before coming down to Earth, they inhabit different villages or towns, and those in the same community share similar tendencies. This means that those who live in the same neighborhood are of a similar spiritual vibration while those residing in distant communities will be quite different. Souls that share a similar spiritual wavelength will naturally be drawn to one another, while those who do not match will find it difficult to be together for very long.

Differences of spiritual genealogy

Souls that belong to a group that values intellect will generally be born clever. On the other hand, those belonging to groups that place more value on sensitivity are born sensitive, and often lack intellectual aptitude. Those who belong to groups that value reason are born with a very logical streak.

These kinds of soul traits are referred to as a person's "temperament" or "character," and there are great differences between different groups of souls. There is difference between what is intelligent in the spiritual sense and what is considered clever from the perspective of this world, so it is difficult to say who is actually intelligent. Here on Earth, schoolteachers assess the intellectual level of students. However, when doing this, they do not really take into account sensitivity, rationality or creativity. Because souls all belong to different groups, it is difficult to assess intellectual ability accurately.

Intelligence—70 percent the influence of the soul, 30 percent the influence of the physical body

Taking the above as a basic premise, I would now like to consider the question of whether intelligence is spiritual or physical in origin. The truth is that it is seventy percent spiritual. The soul enters a baby's body before birth and as a child grows up, the brain gradually takes on the tendencies of the soul. The brain can be likened to a computer that organizes and transmits data, and in the course of a life the soul gradually builds its own machine. So the influence of the soul plays a major role in determining the intelligence of the individual, and can account for about seventy percent of the influence, the remaining thirty percent being the influence of the physical body.

What are the physical influences? There are two physical conditions that assist the development of the brain. The first are the basic substances from which the brain is made. In periods of war, when people suffered from malnutrition, even gifted souls who should have developed into clever people were unable to do so due to a lack of basic nutrition that prevented the brain from growing to its full potential. The environment in which people are raised greatly influences the development of the brain.

The most important nutrient required to promote the growth

of the brain is protein. Protein can be found in soybeans, milk, eggs, fish, meat, etc. and if it is lacking in the diet during the period when the brain is developing, the brain's growth will be stunted and the "machine" will fail to function efficiently. Sugars and oxygen are also necessary for the operation of the brain. These nutritional demands constitute the first factor.

The second factor is connected to training. Even though an individual may be extremely clever as a soul, and may have received an adequate supply of nutrients, for the brain to function efficiently as a "computer," a person needs to learn how to "operate" it; training is required. People who have not made sufficient effort will find that their brain will not develop to its full potential.

No matter how blessed they may be with latent ability, if they do not make the effort to study during the process of growth from child to adult, the brain will not achieve its full potential. Conversely, however, even though a person may not be particularly gifted, if they make an effort, they can make good use of the brain's functions and become clever. So, differences in intelligence are seventy percent the result of the soul's inherent tendencies, and thirty percent the result of physical conditions, and what is learned after birth.

5. It Is Possible to Overcome Hereditary Diseases

Question: *We hear about hereditary diseases, but from a spiritual viewpoint, what is the relationship between genetic inheritance and illness?*

The body as the car, the soul as the driver
Genes represent the blueprint of a body. A child receives this blueprint from its parents and the body is constructed accordingly.

However, having said this, the way in which the body finally takes shape is more than fifty percent the result of post-natal factors. For instance, even if both parents are athletic and endowed with muscular physiques, if their child has never played any sports, the child will not develop that kind of body. Or, if both parents are highly intellectual but their child does not make sufficient effort to study, he or she will not grow up to be like them.

Although people possess a blueprint of sorts, the way in which they finally turn out depends entirely on the individual. If we were to take the car as a metaphor, we could say that the body is the vehicle while the soul is the driver. The way in which a car is driven changes dramatically according to the person who is driving it. Someone who understands the capabilities of the car or who is a very skilled driver will be able to control it brilliantly, whereas a bad driver will be unable to master it, no matter what its potential. Different cars have a different performance potential; however, it is possible for an expert driver to get more out of a low-performance car than a bad driver can out of a powerful one. It is also true that depending on the way in which it is driven and maintained, a car can be either reliable or prone to breakdowns.

Though we are using the metaphor of a car, the same can be said of our physical bodies. Even though a car may be prone to breakdowns, if it is well-serviced and driven with care, it will rarely break down. In the same way, although one may inherit genes that make the body prone to ill-health, with care it is possible to live one's life without serious illness.

Genes are imprinted with a spiritual stamp

There are some things, however, that cannot be avoided simply by taking care. The reason for this is that the genes are imprinted with a spiritual plan. To a certain extent, a person's genes carry within them a person's destiny. Ordinarily, everyone wants to live a long life, but this does not always aid spiritual growth so some people die as children, others in their youth and still others in middle age. People die at different ages, and there are those whose destiny calls for them to die early. The reason is that this experience will provide some kind of learning for their souls.

In these cases, people have a spiritual stamp, the stamp of fate imprinted upon their genes. This is something that is extremely difficult to remove, and as a result, when the person reaches a certain age, they will contract the preordained sickness and die. It may not necessarily be a disease, it may be an accident that brings about their death. However, changes in a person's situation may sometimes result in that person leading a completely different life to the one planned for them. For instance, as a result of having studied the Truth, people may begin to receive direction from a guiding spirit, resulting in a sudden alteration of their plans.

If it were not for this fact, they would have followed the prearranged life plan, facing an illness and dying young. The majority of people who leave this world early do so because it has been preordained in this way. However, in cases where people die as a result of too much alcohol or because they have been reckless about their health, it is impossible to say whether their lives were originally planned that way, although a liking for alcohol may have been imprinted in the genes.

Spiritually speaking, thirty years of age is a milestone
Up until the age of about thirty, the character and physical characteristics of both men and women are largely influenced by what

they have inherited. From this time onward, however, it is the aspects they themselves develop that take on a dominant role in their lives, rather than the traits inherited from their parents. This is most commonly the case. For this reason, after the age of thirty, people no longer bear a close resemblance to their parents, and brothers and sisters can become quite different.

The age of thirty is a milestone in the spiritual sense. After this, you take responsibility for your own actions and are able to change greatly. Your face will change as will your character. This is because you undergo numerous experiences, allowing the true nature of your soul to manifest. Even though you are related by blood to your parents and siblings, the differences between souls gradually become clear.

To finish, I would like to add that from a medical standpoint, you will resemble your parents both physically and in terms of lifestyle, so take precautions to avoid the illnesses they have suffered. With care and effort, it is possible to overcome lifestyle-related illnesses.

6. A Happy Household Can Prevent Child Abuse

Question: *Recently, the abuse of children by parents has become a major social problem. Is there a spiritual influence at work in this kind of child abuse? I am a nurse, so what should I do to avoid negative spiritual influences in my work?*

Negative spiritual influences are at work in persistent child abuse

There are different forms of child abuse and one of the reasons it arises is stress. For example, when a wife is frustrated with her husband but cannot express her feelings toward him because he would quickly resort to violence or verbal abuse, she takes out her stress on her children instead. This is also the result of a father having been treated spitefully by others in the family or in the workplace; although he wants to do something about it, he is powerless against them and so he vents his feelings on children.

While it is common for parents to abuse their children as a result of the stress of their daily lives, it is often the case that they are just giving in to anger. If this kind of child abuse persists, we can almost certainly say that there is some interference by spiritual influences. Parents who abuse their children have invariably come under some sort of negative spiritual influence.

When a person is negatively affected by a stray spirit, they will display clear personality changes. They become pessimistic about everything, and look for external causes for their unhappiness. For example, for a mother, the easiest target for blame is her children, so she begins to think that she is unhappy because her children cause her a lot of trouble. She believes that it is the children who are taking her time and energy, who are a nuisance in terms of her work, and so she takes out her frustrations on them. However, the children are to be pitied because if they are treated like this, it will distort their character.

If a father is violent toward his children, in many cases it is the result of spiritual disturbances, and the cause underlying this can be that he feels unloved by his partner, is suffering a lot of stress at work, or has some sexual frustration (this can also be a cause of violence by a wife). Some men tend to behave in a childish way. If the parents have remarried and one is abusing a child that is not his or her own, this is also a serious problem. These people need to have a firm understanding of the Truth.

Make an effort to create a happy family

In this kind of situation, all that can be done is to fill the home with happiness. Make an effort to find joy in the home. There is no need to fear the presence of stray spirits; they are just like cockroaches and if a place is tidy and brightly lit, they will not come around. Roaches always make their appearance in kitchen garbage, and likewise, stray spirits appear in the dark spots in a family, where complaints and dissatisfaction have accumulated. So it is necessary to bring light to these places and find happiness there.

To achieve this, the support of your spouse and the rest of the family are definitely required. Once you feel that your home is not in an ideal state, all your family members need to join hands and work to make the household a happier place. If you can listen to what your spouse has to say and understand him or her deeply, then you will find that things improve.

If you have some problem with other members of your family, for example, your in-laws, make the effort to discover the best qualities in those people. If the wife asks her mother-in-law not to complain, it will merely make her angry. It is a much better idea to ask her to wait while the wife makes the effort to improve. The mother-in-law's attitude will soften because she will think that although the young wife still does not measure up, she may get better. This kind of effort is necessary.

A supply of light through studying the Truth

What I have to talk about next concerns those who work in the nursing profession. This is a job that creates a lot of stress, and if you are not careful, you will find that you come under negative spiritual influences. There are a lot of people who are affected by spiritual influences in a negative way while taking care of the sick, the elderly or the young, and some of them actually become unstable. For this reason, people involved in this kind of work must be prepared to become a source of an endless supply of love.

Every day before you start work, build up your supply of energy. For instance, before you leave for work each morning, take some time to read a book of the Truth, or listen to a tape or CD of a teaching on the Truth that contains the power of light in its words. If you have taken refuge in the Three Jewels of Buddha, Dharma and Sangha and joined Happy Science, you will have received the sutras and prayer books, *Buddha's Teaching: The Dharma of the Right Mind, Prayers I* and *Prayers II,* so make good use of these. Recite these sutras and prayers, take time to attune the vibration of your mind to heaven, and receive a supply of light.

If you have managed to bring harmony into your heart, it would be a good idea to pray in the morning. If you are involved in nursing, your prayer could consist of something like this: "As I do my work this day I want to become an embodiment of love. Please provide me with the strength to manifest this through-out the day." If you pray for this, you will receive power from the heavenly world and you will be able to make lots of people happier. Nursing is a labor-intensive profession; it is easy to be influenced by the unhappiness of others, so I would like everyone in the nursing profession to study the Truth and devise ways of keeping their inner light strong.

7. Secrets for Overcoming a Short Temper and Developing Patience

Question: *My family often tells me that I am short-tempered and too hard on others. How should I go about overcoming this and becoming more patient?*

Be aware of the fact you are not perfect

Short-tempered people have a tendency to perfectionism and are extremely anxious; moreover, they look for the same high standards and perfectionism in others as well as in themselves. As a result, they become short-tempered, anger easily and are always on edge. For this kind of person, what is important is to realize the true nature of humankind; they need to understand that they themselves are not perfect. If they are incapable of realizing this, they will be given opportunities to allow them to come to this conclusion as a result of external events. Something is sure to happen to wound their pride.

Perfectionists are people who dream of doing things perfectly, and often they have succumbed to the illusion that they themselves are indeed perfect. In other words, they are people who aim for things that are beyond their ability to attain. The higher they reach, the more pain they will feel when they fall. When something occurs to teach them that they are not perfect, the shock affects them deeply. It may be the result of some personal failure, or they may have this experience through receiving help from other people in a time of illness or some other misfortune. This kind of experience will allow them to realize their own imperfections. Some kind of failure will occur to make them see they are not perfect, resulting in their becoming kinder to others.

Acquire knowledge and experience

Secondly, it is important to work on yourself. Refined people who have much knowledge are not short-tempered. There may be people who believe themselves to be cultured but who are nonetheless short-tempered. However, truly knowledgeable people are never short-tempered.

The reason why knowledgeable people are not short-tempered is that the gap of awareness that exists between them and others is too vast for arguments to occur. For instance, a schoolteacher will not get into a serious argument with one of his pupils. In the same way, truly knowledgeable people would not be able to speak harshly to someone who is at a lower level than themselves. Because they know that the other person does not yet understand what they are talking about, they will speak more simply. So, studying more and acquiring knowledge and experience are effective ways of overcoming a short temper.

Have faith

The third method of curing a short temper is none other than having faith. When a person enters the world of faith and starts to think about God or Buddha, he or she becomes incapable of judging others from a human perspective. Perfectionists are self-confident and rate themselves too highly, but if they think about God or Buddha every day, they will discover that they are actually very small beings. They will see themselves as a single speck in the vastness of the universe. For this reason, they are no longer capable of arrogance and cannot help but be humble.

People who learn humility in the face of God or Buddha find it impossible to be short-tempered with others. They realize that even an imperfect person such as themselves has been given the gift of life, blessed with a life; so they cannot bring themselves to treat others harshly.

Here I have presented three ways of overcoming a short temper. The first is to realize that you are not perfect, the second is to cultivate yourself and the third is to have faith. For those who wish to engage in serious spiritual development to transform themselves, the seminars on the Eightfold Path that are held at our meditation centers are highly recommended. Self-reflection in connection with Right Thought and Right Speech are particularly important.

8. How to Expand Your Capacity to Love

Question: *Please tell me how to expand the capacity to love and how to develop my ability to talk to others about the Truth in a way that is appropriate for each person.*

Understanding is synonymous with loving

With regard to love, what is fundamentally important is to understand others. To understand someone means virtually the same as loving that person. When people are unable to love it is because they cannot understand. You may ask yourself why you are unable to love a certain person, but the answer is that you cannot understand that person. When you can understand someone, you will be able to love them.

In the case of married couples, too, if one partner does not love the other, it is because they cannot understand their partner. This is generally true. If they could understand the person, then they could also love. A husband and wife each have their own complaints and explain them to the other, but because each is unable to understand the other and unable to forgive the other, conflict arises. If people can understand each other, they will be able to love.

Develop the ability to understand through experience and knowledge

The same is true when you try to convey the Truth to others in the way that is most appropriate to each; the extent to which you are able to understand the other person is of vital importance. If you are only able to talk to people of the same type as yourself, the extent to which you are able to expound the Truth will be very limited.

It is easy to talk to people who accept you. If you talk to those who think of you as a good and trustworthy person, it is easy for them to appreciate what you have to say. However, it is much harder to talk to someone who is different. There are people you have to struggle with to make them listen, which requires as much energy as smashing through a wall with a hammer. There are even those who have never had any chance to study the Truth in past lives and who will resist believing what you tell them at all costs.

The first requisite when enlarging your capacity to love is to gain the ability to understand. This can be achieved through effort. Through gaining experience and increasing your knowledge, you will become capable of understanding others. If you can understand someone, you will be able to love that person. Likewise, if you feel that someone understands you, you will feel that you are loved.

Listen carefully to what others say

In order to understand others, it is important that you listen carefully to what they have to say. By doing this, you will find that your understanding will grow. It is very common for people to force their opinions on others without bothering to listen to what others have to say. This is true in the home as well. Even if you do not do anything else, just listen carefully to what your partner has to say, and you will find that lots of problems will be solved by the mere act of listening. When your partner is beset by numerous worries that cannot be easily solved, try to listen to what he or she has to say and that may well be the end of the matter. So if you want to understand others, improve your ability to listen. A willingness to listen to what others have to say is also an expression of a loving heart.

The same is true of conveying the Truth to others on a one-to-one basis. What is important is how much you are able to understand others, how deeply you are aware of the huge variety of people that exists in this world. In the same way that there are many different sorts of fish in a lake, there are also many different types of people and each type has its own worries and ways of worrying. For instance, there are some who soon get over their problems if they receive encouragement, while others, even when offered encouragement, will feel that they cannot keep up and even be driven to commit suicide.

The only way to be able to understand what type of person you are dealing with is to build up your knowledge through experience. To achieve this end, it is important that you make the effort to understand others.

The metaphor of the lotus flower

About two thousand five hundred years ago, Shakyamuni Buddha used the parable of the lotus flower to explain the basic attitude for conveying the Truth. He taught in this way: "Some lotuses extend their stems up out of the water and produce beautiful, big flowers. These lotuses bloom by themselves. They are complete in themselves, there is nothing that you have to do to help them. On the other hand, some lotuses remain at the bottom of the pond, buried in mud, unable to rise above the surface of the water. These are extremely difficult to bring to flower and great patience is required.

"However, there are lotuses lying just below the surface of the water, which only have to grow a fraction more to rise up out of it. If you make the effort to help these lotuses, they will succeed in lifting their heads and turning into magnificent blooms."

Know what sort of person you are talking to

The basis of conveying the Truth is to help the third type of lotus blossoms that the parable describes, those that need only a gentle nudge to awaken. People who are about to emerge from out of the water, and who need make only a little more effort or need only a little more help will blossom beautifully with a little outside assistance.

On the other hand, there are people who bloom by themselves, who when asked if they want happiness will reply that they are already quite happy, and satisfied with their lives. It is a fact that there are people who live wonderful lives, and although they may follow the words of people they respect, they will not be convinced by the words of people who seem less happy than themselves. Unless these people become interested in religion in their own right, they may well claim to have no need of it.

There are also others who lead selfish lives and no matter what anyone may say to them, it simply rolls off them like water off a duck's back. The Laws of Truth mean nothing to people like this and it is extremely difficult to convey the Truth to these kinds of people. They will not learn the Truth until an opportunity presents itself; for instance, until they become ill, a loved one dies, their children create problems or their business goes bankrupt. When this kind of misfortune happens, they find themselves in need of the teachings so then it is necessary to give them knowledge of the Truth appropriate to their situation.

The people who most need guidance are those almost within the reach of the Truth and who are about to create a wonderful life for themselves. Shakyamuni taught that these are the ones for whom the teachings are both important and necessary, and that remains true to this day. If you make the effort to differentiate between these three types, I am sure your efforts to convey the Truth will be successful.

Postscript

More than seventeen years have now passed since I founded Happy Science with a strong wish to bring true happiness to as many people as possible. I have published well over three hundred books in Japanese, and a total of over one hundred million copies have been printed. The number of people who have heard my lectures, either directly or indirectly, would easily exceed ten million.

Nonetheless, I believe there is a value in publishing this book in the world today. Philosophy must always be available in a form that is easy to understand and be circulated back to the living or it becomes lifeless. It is because this book gives practical examples put forward by real people that I have been able to write purposefully and in such an impassioned way. Having read it repeatedly, I find sections of this book that even I, the author, can use as a guide in my own life and so I am sure that for people who are coming into contact with the Truth for the first time, it will be like coming across a gold mine.

For those who wish to learn more about happiness and appreciate a logical approach, I recommend *The Laws of Happiness*, which I hope you will also enjoy reading.

Ryuho Okawa
Founder and CEO
Happy Science Group

About the Author

Ryuho Okawa, founder of Happy Science, Kofuku-no-Kagaku in Japan, has devoted his life to the exploration of the Truth and ways to happiness.

He was born in 1956 in Tokushima, Japan. He graduated from the University of Tokyo. In March 1981, he received his higher calling and awakened to the hidden part of his consciousness, El Cantare. After working at a major Tokyo-based trading house and studying international finance at the Graduate Center of the City University of New York, he established Happy Science in 1986.

Since then, he has been designing spiritual workshops for people from all walks of life, from teenagers to business executives. He is known for his wisdom, compassion and commitment to educating people to think and act in spiritual and religious ways.

He is a best-selling author of 100 million books sold worldwide, and has published titles such as *The Laws of the Sun*, *The Golden Laws*, *The Laws of Eternity*, *The Science of Happiness*, and *The Essence of Buddha*. He has also produced successful feature-length films (including animations) based on his works.

The members of Happy Science follow the path he teaches, ministering to people who need help by sharing his teachings.

Lantern Books by Ryuho Okawa

The Laws of the Sun: *Discover the Origin of Your Soul*
978-1-93005-162-1

The Golden Laws: *History through the Eyes of the Eternal Buddha*
978-1-59056-241-3

The Laws of Eternity: *Unfolding the Secrets of the Multidimensional Universe*
1-930051-63-8

The Starting Point of Happiness:
A Practical and Intuitive Guide to Discovering Love, Wisdom, and Faith
978-1-59056-312-0

Love, Nurture, and Forgive: *A Handbook to Add a New Richness to Your Life*
1-930051-78-6

An Unshakable Mind: *How to Overcome Life's Difficulties*
1-930051-77-8

The Origin of Love: *On the Beauty of Compassion*
978-1-59056-313-7

Invincible Thinking: *There Is No Such Thing As Defeat*
1-59056-051-5

Guideposts to Happiness: *Prescriptions for a Wonderful Life*
978-1-59056-314-4

The Philosophy of Progress: *Higher Thinking for Developing Infinite Prosperity*
1-59056-057-4

The Laws of Happiness: *Four Principles for a Successful Life*
978-1-59056-094-9

Ten Principles of Universal Wisdom:
The Truth of Happiness, Enlightenment, and the Creation of an Ideal World
1-59056-094-9

Tips to Find Happiness:
Creating a Harmonious Home for You, Your Spouse, and Your Children
978-1-59056-315-1

Order at www.lanternbooks.com

What is Happy Science?

Happy Science is an organization of people who aim to cultivate their souls and deepen their love and wisdom through learning and practicing the teachings (the Truth) of Ryuho Okawa. Happy Science spreads the light of Truth, with the aim of creating an ideal world on Earth.

Members learn the Truth through books, lectures, and seminars to acquire knowledge of a spiritual view of life and the world. They also practice meditation and self-reflection daily, based on the Truth they have learned. This is the way to develop a deeper understanding of life and build characters worthy of being leaders in society who can contribute to the development of the world.

Events and Seminars

There are regular events and seminars held at your local temple. These include practicing meditation, watching video lectures, study group sessions, seminars and book events. All these offer a great opportunity to meet like-minded friends on the same path to happiness and for further soul development. By being an active participant at your local temples you will be able to:

- Know the purpose and meaning of life
- Know the true meaning of love and create better relationships
- Learn how to meditate to achieve serenity of mind
- Learn how to overcome life's challenges

...and much more

International Seminars

International seminars are held in Japan each year where members have a chance to deepen their enlightenment and meet friends from all over the world who are studying Happy Science's teachings.

Happy Science Monthly Publications

Happy Science has been publishing monthly magazines for English readers around the world since 1994. Each issue contains Master Okawa's latest lectures, words of wisdom, stories of remarkable life-changing experiences, up-to-date news from around the globe, in-depth explanations of the different aspects of Happy Science, movie and book reviews, and much more to guide readers to a happier life.

Hundreds of interesting back-issues of our monthly publications are available at your nearest temple.

You can pick up the latest issue from your nearest temple or subscribe to have them delivered *(please contact your nearest temple from the contacts page)*. Happy Science Monthly is available in many other languages too, including Portuguese, Spanish, French, German, Chinese, and Korean.

Our Welcome e-Booklet

You can read our Happy Science Welcome Introductory Booklet and find out the basics of Happy Science, testimonies from members and even register with us:

http://content.yudu.com/Library/A1e44v/HappyScienceIntro

If you have any questions, please email us at:
inquiry@happy-science.org

Contacts

**Find more information about Happy Science
by visiting the websites below**

Global Website
www.happy-science.org

Japan
www.kofuku-no-kagaku.or.jp/en
Tokyo
1-6-7 Togoshi, Shinagawa,
Tokyo, 142-0041 Japan
Tel: 81-3-6384-5770
Fax: 81-3-6384-5776
tokyo@happy-science.org

United States of America
New York
www.happyscience-ny.org
79 Franklin Street,
New York, NY 10013, U.S.A.
Tel: 1-212-343-7972
Fax: 1-212-343-7973
ny@happy-science.org

Los Angeles
www.happyscience-la.org
1590 E. Del Mar Blvd.,
Pasadena, CA 91106, U.S.A.
Tel: 1-626-395-7775
Fax: 1-626-395-7776
la@happy-science.org

San Francisco
www.happyscience-sf.org
525 Clinton St.,
Redwood City, CA
94062, U.S.A
Tel: 1-650-363-2777
Fax: same
sf@happy-science.org

New York East
nyeast@happy-science.org

New Jersey
nj@happy-science.org

Florida
www.happyscience-fl.org
florida@happy-science.org

Chicago
chicago@happy-science.org

San Diego
sandiego@happy-science.org

Atlanta
atlanta@happy-science.org

Hawaii
www.happyscience-hi.org
hi@happy-science.org

Kauai
kauai-hi@happy-science.org

Canada
Toronto
www.happy-science.ca
toronto@happy-science.org

Vancouver
vancouver@happy-science.org

Europe
London
www.happyscience-eu.org
3 Margaret Street, London
W1W 8RE, United Kingdom
Tel: 44-20-7323-9255
Fax: 44-20-7323-9344
eu@happy-science.org

Oceania
Sydney
www.happyscience.org.au
sydney@happy-science.org

East Sydney
bondi@happy-science.org

Melbourne
melbourne@happy-science.org

New Zealand
newzealand@happy-science.org

To find more Happy Science
locations worldwide, go to
www.happy-science.org/en/
contact-us

Want to Know More?

Thank you for choosing this book. If you would like to receive further information about titles by Ryuho Okawa, please send the following information either by fax, post or e-mail to your nearest Happy Science Branch.

1. Title Purchased

_____

2. Please let us know your impression of this book.

_____

_____

3. Are you interested in receiving a catalog of Ryuho Okawa's books?

      Yes ❏   No ❏

4. Are you interested in receiving Happy Science Monthly?

      Yes ❏   No ❏

Name : Mr / Mrs / Ms / Miss: _____

Addres : _____

_____

_____

Phone: _____

Email: _____

Thank you for your interest in Lantern Books.